# Book of Ephesians: Bible Studies

# Books by Paul J. Bucknell

*Allowing the Bible to speak to our lives today!*

- Overcoming Anxiety: Finding Peace, Discovering God
- Reaching Beyond Mediocrity: Being an Overcomer
- The Life Core: Discovering the Heart of Great Training
- The Godly Man: When God Touches a Man's Life
- Redemption Through the Scriptures
- Godly Beginnings for the Family
- Principles and Practices of Biblical Parenting
- Building a Great Marriage
- Christian Premarital Counseling Manual for Counselors
- Relational Discipleship: Cross Training
- Running the Race: Overcoming Lusts
- Genesis: The Book of Foundations
- Book of Romans: The Living Commentary
- Book of Romans: Bible Study Questions
- Book of Ephesians: Bible Studies
- Walking with Jesus: Abiding in Christ
- Inductive Bible Studies in Titus
- 1 Peter Bible Study Questions: Living in a Fallen World.
- Take Your Next Step into Ministry
- Training Leaders for Ministry
- Study Guide for Jonah: Understanding God's Heart
  - ➡ Check out these valuable resources at www.foundationsforfreedom.net

# Book of Ephesians:
# Bible Studies

## Paul J. Bucknell

Book of Ephesians: Bible Studies

Copyright ©2014 Paul J. Bucknell

ISBN-10: 1619930374

ISBN-13: 978-1-61993-037-7

Also in digital book formats:

ISBN-10: 1619930250

ISBN-13: 978-1-61993-025-4

www.foundationsforfreedom.net

3276 Bainton St., Pittsburgh, PA 15212, USA

The NASB version is used unless otherwise stated.
New American Standard Bible ©1960, 1995 used by permission, Lockman Foundation www.lockman.org.

All rights reserved. Limited production is acceptable without prior permission for home and educational use. For extensive reproduction or questions please contact Paul Bucknell at info@foundationsforfreedom.net.

# Introduction

## Stepping into the Book of Ephesians

The Book of Ephesians opens up before us a panorama of God's grand scheme of redemption, a view of His eternal plan, reaching from the depths of our depravity to the eternal heavens where Christ dwells and His people now reign with Him. The apostle is fully absorbed in the seamless glory of God's eternal salvation plan. These Bible studies are designed to help us meet this glorious God, grasp the awe of His redemption plan and build up the faith of His people. The topics are very wide describing spiritual powers active in our world, our old nature, the riches of our salvation in Christ, the astonishing spiritual armor to daily scenes of marriage, parenting and work.

These Bible studies are intentionally more thorough to discover the richness Paul the Apostle intended for us to receive in this book. The passages discuss fewer verses with greater depth, at times only targeting several verses, fostering biblical mediation. Each study is aimed to inspire us to further comprehend the great meaning of God's redemptive work in our world and our personal lives.

## Hints for group Bible studies

These thirty studies are designed to deepen a person or group's understanding and joy of the Book of Ephesians. While personal Bible studies are less restricted by time, small groups often are, so these studies might need to be combined or condensed to study the entire book within a limited frame of time. For instance, shorter passages can be blended together. (The docx format assists in reformatting the studies – found in the BFF NT Digital Library.) Prepare better group studies by discarding less relevant questions to make room for the most important ones depending on the group's needs, focusing on only one major theme for each study.

A 'kickoff question' is supplied at the beginning of each study. Feel free to use (or not use) this lighter question to get people pointed in the direction of the suggested theme given in the scripture passage.

Each study uses the following categories of questions:

- Bible questions: The verse at hand supplies the answer. The verse number is given to pinpoint the verse under scrutiny. We regularly use the NASB (New American Standard Bible), though not always, since other versions at times bring out the meaning more clearly.

- Connection questions: These broaden the understanding of the text by connecting what Paul has said to our own experiences.

- Application questions: The aim here is to soften our hearts to shape our lives by God's eternal truths. If the Word of God cannot reach our hearts, then the study has largely lost its power.

- Since the Spirit enlightens our hearts, a critical part of Bible study is to pray while studying and making sure to conclude in prayer so to fully integrate these truths into our daily lives.

- Advanced study questions: Unlike the above questions, these are sectioned separately at the end of each study because they require more time and study, but they allow us deepen the impact of God's Word on our life and theology. They are well worth the time and energy. Some of them are appropriate to use in group Bible study if they match up with the chosen theme.

## Final thoughts

I have written hundreds of Bible studies, and yet this Ephesian study holds a special place in my heart, reminding me of the many steps God used to change my life and deepen my commitment to Him. It is so easy to allow the events of the day to be lifted above God's glorious purposes to make God's people vibrant with His hope, joy and love. May God brilliantly restore our focus on Christ and His glorious purposes for His church and our individual lives!

Enjoy this unending adventure in discovering God's glorious ways.

Rev. Paul J. Bucknell, December 2014

Pittsburgh, PA USA

# Tribute

God graciously invites us on this journey through the Book of Ephesians to further discover and revel in His glorious person and plans. Grace well describes our lives–receiving the good that we do not deserve. Oh, that we could better swallow our pride and be wholly enraptured with His presence! Blessed be the God of all grace!

*Now to him who is able to do far more*

*abundantly than all that we ask or think,*

*according to the power at work within us, to*

*him be glory in the church and in Christ Jesus*

*throughout all generations, forever and ever.*

*Amen. (Eph 3:20-21 ESB)*

# Acknowledgement

We are very grateful to Kurt Jorgensen who carefully read this manuscript through and made corrections.

# Table of Contents

### Ephesians 1:1-3
*Living as Saints* ................................................................... 15

### Ephesians 1:4-6
*Chosen and Precious* ............................................................ 19

### Ephesians 1:7-10
*A Grand World View* ........................................................... 23

### Ephesians 1:11-14
*A Glorious Life* .................................................................... 27

### Ephesians 1:15-17
*A Model of Prayer* ............................................................... 31

### Ephesians 1:18-23
*Penetrating Prayers* .............................................................. 35

### Ephesians 2:1-3
*The Need for Grace* ............................................................. 41

### Ephesians 2:4-7
*God's Great Mercy* ............................................................... 45

Ephesians 2:8-10
*God's Awesome Plan for You*......................49

Ephesians 2:11-18
*He Himself is Our Peace*.........................55

Ephesians 2:19-22
*No Longer Strangers* ............................61

Ephesians 3:1-10
*The Purpose of the Gospel* ......................67

Ephesians 3:11-19
*God's Greater Purposes*.........................73

Ephesians 3:20-21
*Extraordinary Glory*............................77

Ephesians 4:1-3
*Preserving the Unity*...........................81

Ephesians 4:4-10
*Unity and Harmony* .............................85

Ephesians 4:11-16
*God's Goal for the Church*......................91

Ephesians 4:17-24
*Life Transformation*............................97

### Ephesians 4:25
*Pure Living (Part 1)* ............................................................ *103*

### Ephesians 4:26-32
*Pure Living (Part 2)* ............................................................ *107*

### Ephesians 5:1-7
*Pure Living (Part 3)* ............................................................ *111*

### Ephesians 5:8-14
*Children of Light* ................................................................. *117*

### Ephesians 5:15-21
*Filled With the Spirit* ........................................................... *121*

### Ephesians 5:22-30
*Improving One's Marriage* .................................................. *127*

### Ephesians 5:31-33
*The Picture of Marriage* ...................................................... *133*

### Ephesians 6:1-4
*Family Matters* .................................................................... *139*

### Ephesians 6:5-9
*Responsibilities and Opportunities* ..................................... *143*

### Ephesians 6:10-13
*Engaged in War* ................................................................... *147*

### Ephesians 6:14-17
*Spiritual Armor* ................................................................. *153*

### Ephesians 6:18-24
*Power in Prayer* ................................................................. *159*

## Appendix 1: Bible Study Chart

## Appendix 2: About the Author

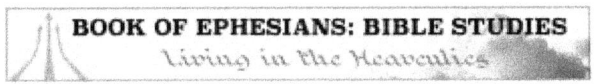

# Ephesians 1:1-3

# LIVING AS SAINTS

How awesome it is to receive a message from God! This letter, although originally written to the church in Ephesus, is extended to us who are "faithful in Christ Jesus."

➡ What was the last letter/email you wrote? What was it about?

## Basic Study Questions on Ephesians 1:1-3

> ¹ Paul, an apostle of Christ Jesus by the will of God, to the saints who are at Ephesus, and who are faithful in Christ Jesus: ² Grace to you and peace from God our Father and the Lord Jesus Christ. ³ Blessed be the God and Father of our Lord Jesus Christ, who has blessed us with every spiritual blessing in the heavenly places in Christ. (Eph 1:1-3)

1. Who wrote the Book of Ephesians? How do you know? (1:1)

2. What made Paul an apostle (1)? From your biblical knowledge what is an apostle? What are three of Paul's significant experiences that contributed to his experience as an apostle? (See the Book of Acts for this development.)

3. Why do you think the letter was named the Book of Ephesians (1:1)?

4. What are the two ways that Paul describes these Christians in Ephesus (1:1)? What does the first term mean? Look it up in a Bible dictionary and compare your answer.

5. What might it mean to be 'faithful in Christ' (1:1)? Does it refer to our coming to believe in Christ or our growing faith in Christ, or both?

6. What are the two things that God the Father has given to His people (1:2)? Define each of them in this context.

7. Observe how many times the word 'Christ' is used in verses 1:1-3. What does "Christ" mean? What is the slight difference of meaning with each phrase?

8. Identify the three derivatives from the root word 'blessed' used in verse 3. Why might Paul write the sentence in this way?

9. Use verse 1:3 to answer, "What place does God the Father and the Lord Jesus Christ have in our salvation?"

10. What is a spiritual blessing (3)? How is it different from earthly blessings?

11. Since all the spiritual blessings are in the heavenlies, it is important for these blessings to affect our present earthly lives. Name a few ways spiritual blessings presently impact your life here.

12. Give 3-5 adjectives to describe what God has done for us (1-3)? Provide another 3-5 adjectives that describe how we should respond to Him?

13. Considering the blessings that God has given us in Christ, explain the reasons we tend to doubt the sufficiency of God's resources for our present or future circumstance.

## Advanced Study Questions on Ephesians 1:1-3

1. Why is Paul writing this letter to the Ephesians? (See Acts 19 for background.)

2. The words 'at Ephesus' are not in the earliest manuscripts. We are not positive the words are there. It could have been left out as it was passed on to other churches. Study up on the pros and cons of having the words 'at Ephesus' in the original letter.

3. Reflect on your periods of worship. Do you really worship Him like Paul does in verse 3? What great things do you think, say or sing of the Lord?

4. What does heavenlies (literally) or 'heavenly places' mean? Explore the five times it is used in the Book of Ephesians.

5. Share and pray about three ways you would want God to show you more truths about these spiritual blessings so that you can grow to be a stronger saint.

**BOOK OF EPHESIANS: BIBLE STUDIES**
Living in the Heavenlies

# Ephesians 1:4-6
## CHOSEN AND PRECIOUS

Take a deep and penetrating look of the truths unveiled before us here! How would we know these things if the Lord did not tell us?

➡ Did you have a sense of being loved as you grew up? What is one way it could have been better?

## Basic Study Questions on Ephesians 1:4-6

> 4 Just as He chose us in Him before the foundation of the world, that we should be holy and blameless before Him. In love 5 He predestined us to adoption as sons through Jesus Christ to Himself, according to the kind intention of His will, 6 to the praise of the glory of His grace, which He freely bestowed on us in the Beloved. (Eph 1:4-6)

1. Read Ephesians 1:3. What is it that God has said to have given us?

2. The spiritual blessings that the Lord has given to His people are listed in the following verses (verses 3-14). Name those spiritual blessings listed in Ephesians 1:4-6.

3. We will look at each blessing individually though they are interrelated. The first one is that the Lord has chosen us in "Him." Who does the 'us' refer to? How do you know? Who does the 'Him' refer to?

4. Think of shopping at a book or food store. Why do you choose to buy or use certain items? Might this be the same reason God has chosen us? How do you know?

5. When did the Lord make this choice (1:4)? What are the implications of choosing us then and not later after we were born?

6. What was His purpose of choosing His people (1:4)? Are we not sinners? How can this be?

7. Sometimes a person fails God. He wants to give up on following Christ. How could you use this teaching about "choosing us in Christ before the foundation of the world" to encourage another Christian to encourage another Christian to keep following the Lord?

8. Is it wrong for a man to choose one woman for his wife? Why or why not? God's choice of us should cause our hearts to celebrate and be glad, much like a bride's. How do you respond to the Lord's choice for you? Do you feel treasured?

# Ephesians 1:4-6 Chosen and Precious

9. How does the Lord treat His people (1:5)? Would it be appropriate to conclude that God wants to greatly bless His people?

10. What does it mean for the Lord to predestine His people (1:5)?

11. Is there a difference between choosing (1:4) and predestinating us 1:(5)?

12. What was the purpose of this predestination (1:5)? What might be the long term implications of this?

13. The topic of predestination (1:5) can lead to heated discussion. Why is this so?

14. What is the ultimate purpose of election and predestination (examine 1:6 for your answer)? What is the good that we receive from it (1:6)?

## Advanced Study Questions for Ephesians 1:4-6

1. Notice that it says, "He chose us in Christ before the foundation of the world" (1:4) and "predestined us...through Jesus Christ" (1:5), people rather than things or events. Do you like the security of being the Lord's and knowing that nothing can separate you from the love of God which is in Christ (Romans 8:38-39)? Or are you still trying to

acquire this confidence? What difference does this security have on your life?

2. How do you treat family members different from those who are not part of your family? What are the implications of being adopted into God's family (1:5)?

3. Why would God want praise raised for "the glory of His grace" (1:6)? Is this right and good? Is it inappropriate? Explain.

4. Verse 6 says that the Lord "freely bestowed" on us in His beloved. What is it that He has given to us? What does Paul want us to understand by the term "freely"?

5. Study both perspectives: Calvinism and Arminianism. Which do you think Ephesians 1 supports? Why? (Refer: Roman 8:29-30.)

6. Close this time by joining Paul in giving thanks for expressing His kindness to His people reflecting the awesome ways He has chosen and predestined us to be His in Christ.

**BOOK OF EPHESIANS: BIBLE STUDIES**

*Living in the Heavenlies*

# Ephesians 1:7-10
## A GRAND WORLD VIEW

A glorious and very real spiritual world surrounds each of us. May God open our eyes to see this reality and live lives empowered by His truth.

➡ Briefly share when the cross began to be important to you.

## Basic Study Questions on Ephesians 1:7-10

> 7 In Him we have redemption through His blood, the forgiveness of our trespasses, according to the riches of His grace 8 which He lavished on us. In all wisdom and insight 9 He made known to us the mystery of His will, according to His kind intention which He purposed in Him 10 with a view to an administration suitable to the fullness of the times, that is, the summing up of all things in Christ, things in the heavens and things on the earth. In Him. (Eph 1:7-10)

1. Who does the 'in Him' in verse 7 refer to? Underline the other places "His," "He," "Him" are used in these verses.

2. What does redemption mean (1:7)? Use a Bible dictionary as needed.

3. Is redemption a forward or past event? How do you know and what are the implications of this?

4. Explain the connection between Christ's blood and redemption.

5. What are the trespasses that are referred to here in verse 7? What is the spiritual significance of these trespasses and why do they need to be forgiven?

6. Let's connect all the significant words: Him (Jesus), redemption, blood, trespasses and forgiveness. How are they all related? Have you found this true in your life? Please elaborate.

7. In what sense are God's rich grace poured out upon our lives? Upon whose lives is this grace poured out? What added meaning does the word 'lavish' have (verse 1:8)?

8. What might the mystery of His will refer to in verse 9? Are there clues to its meaning from the context? Explain.

Ephesians 1:7-10 A Grand World View          25

9. Verse 8 mentions it is "in his wisdom and insight made known" that the Lord carried out his great redemptive program. Share two aspects of God's marvelous redemptive plan from this greater context. {Redemption Through the Scriptures goes through the Bible revealing the steps of redemption in chronological order.}

10. Would you say you understand the "mystery of His will" (made known to us 1:9)? (Hint: Who is Jesus and why did He die on the cross?)

11. Verse 10 speaks about the full declaration of God's plan. What does it include?

## Advanced Study Questions For Ephesians 1:7-10

1. Often when a person is asked about going to heaven, he or she answers by, "I hope so." This usually reflects their confidence or lack thereof of pleasing God based on their own efforts. From these verses explain what confidence believers should have in gaining eternal life and upon what basis one's confidence should be founded.

2. What do Mormons, Muslims and Jehovah Witnesses put their confidence in?

3. Consider the term "covered in white," symbolizing the attainment of God's righteousness in Christ. Trace the notion of "covering" through the scripture and discuss its development.

4. Does the "riches of His grace" overwhelm you? How or how not? Should they?

5. Verse ten says, "summing up of all things in Christ, things in the heavens and things on the earth." What does Paul mean by this? Feel free to refer to outside sources, but if so, use at least two illustrations.

**BOOK OF EPHESIANS: BIBLE STUDIES**

*Living in the Heavenlies*

# Ephesians 1:11-14
## A GLORIOUS LIFE

The follower of Jesus lives surrounded by the abounding presence and promises of God. It is not just what Jesus has done on the cross, but unending promises for what lies ahead for those in Christ.

➡ Name one article belonging to your parents that you would like passed on to you and your family. Why?

## Basic Study Questions For Ephesians 1:11-14

> 10 In Him 11 also we have obtained an inheritance, having been predestined according to His purpose who works all things after the counsel of His will, 12 to the end that we who were the first to hope in Christ would be to the praise of His glory. 13 In Him, you also, after listening to the message of truth, the gospel of your salvation-having also believed, you were sealed in Him with the Holy Spirit of promise, 14 who is given as a pledge of our inheritance, with a view to the redemption of God's own possession, to the praise of His glory. (Eph 1:11-14)

1. What is an inheritance and how is it obtained? (1:11) How is it that we get an inheritance "in Him" (1:10-11; Hint see v.13)?

2. What is predestination? What does verse 11 says about this topic? Is it true that God's people have been predestined? By what are they predestined?

3. What does the "counsel of His will" refer to (1:11)? Would you say that God has a grand plan, then, from which He works out everything? Explain your answer from this verse.

4. For what purpose was this great redemption plan executed (1:12)? Who does the "first to hope in Christ" refer to? Does this exclude those who believed in Christ later (like ourselves)? Explain.

5. In verse 13 Paul switches from 'we' to 'you.' Why might he do this?

6. Read verse 13 aloud. What does the "message of truth" refer to? How important is it that people hear the Word of God to believe?

7. What do you think Paul was specifically thinking in verse 13 when he said, "the gospel of your salvation?" Or in other words, what truths do you think a person needs to know to become a believer?

8. The word 'believe' means different things to people. Paul uses it to describe a believer, a follower of Jesus. Do you think everyone who raises his or her hand at an evangelism event is saved? Why or why not? Use this verse as reference.

Ephesians 1:11-14 A Glorious Life

9. Upon believing in Christ, what happens to the new believer (13)? Do you think this is a one time thing or can occur repeatedly? Why or why not?

10. Who is the Holy Spirit (13)? Read John 16:7-14 for additional insight.

11. Why do you think Paul uses the phrase "Holy Spirit of promise" (13)?

12. What is a pledge (14)? How is the Holy Spirit a pledge?

13. Read verses 13-14 again. From these verses alone, would you say that the Holy Spirit is given to all believers? Explain your answer.

14. What is God's final purpose for the redemption of His people (14)? How does God bring glory to Himself through carrying out His salvation plan?

# Advanced Study Questions for Ephesians 1:11-14

1. How do earthly and spiritual inheritances differ? Which is of greater value?

2. Predestination in its various forms is used only in six times in the Bible (Ac 4:28; Ro 8:29,30; 1 Cor 2:7; Eph 1:5,11). What do these verses state about predestination? Explore the meaning of predestination considering John 3:16 and Acts 17:30-31.

3. Do a brief review of these verses on the Holy Spirit. In what ways would you say that the Holy Spirit should affect our lives now? Start with these verses.

4. The order of salvation is an important part of the study of theology. What insight do we gain from verse 13? Place the various aspects of salvation in chronological order.

5. Why do some believe that the Holy Spirit can be experienced in more fullness? What do they mean by this? Upon what verses do they base their conclusion? Do you think these verses teach this? Explain.

6. A pledge is a downpayment, a portion of all that is to come. Spend five minutes reflecting on what else might come, knowing that the Holy Spirit is now given as our pledge. Share your thoughts below.

**BOOK OF EPHESIANS: BIBLE STUDIES**
*Living in the Heavenlies*

# Ephesians 1:15-17
## A MODEL OF PRAYER

Learning how to pray and then putting that knowledge into practice form key strategies for a strong spiritual life. In these few verses we can discover much from the apostle.

➡ Do you remember your first prayers? What did you find most significant when you learned God actually heard your prayers in Jesus?

## Basic Study Questions on Ephesians 1:15-17

> ¹⁵ For this reason I too, having heard of the faith in the Lord Jesus which exists among you, and your love for all the saints, ¹⁶ do not cease giving thanks for you, while making mention of you in my prayers; ¹⁷ that the God of our Lord Jesus Christ, the Father of glory, may give to you a spirit of wisdom and of revelation in the knowledge of Him. (Eph 1:15-17)

1. What are the two things Paul heard about these Ephesian believers (1:15)?

2. What does each of them mean? What do you think he might have heard?

3. What is Paul's response to his hearing about them (1:16)?

4. What do you think Paul meant when he said he did, "not cease giving thanks for you (them)"? How can he do this continually? (The NIV reads, "I have not stopped giving thanks for you.")

5. Who is Paul praying for in Ephesians 1:16? Do you pray for particular people or the church as a whole? Explain.

6. How did Paul pray for them (1:17)?

7. Who does Paul ask so that certain things would be done on behalf of the Ephesian believers (1:17)? Why is it that so many Christians pray to Jesus, the Holy Spirit or to Mary instead of God the Father? Is it wrong? Why or why not?

8. Let's go back and look at the two things Paul asked for (1:17). What does 'a spirit of wisdom' mean? Who in the Bible had wisdom? What was it used for? Why do you think Paul asked for this?

Ephesians 1:15-17 A Model of Prayer                                33

9. What now is the second thing Paul asks for? What does 'spirit ... of revelation in the knowledge of Him' mean? Who might 'Him' refer to?

10. What is the difference between asking for knowledge and 'revelation in the knowledge of Him'? Have you ever asked this for yourself? How about for others? Spend some time praying for at least three people, including yourself, for these two things.

11. Review your habit of praying for others (intercessory prayers). How could you improve the quality or time spent praying for others?

## Advanced Study Questions for Ephesians 1:15-17

1. By taking a close look at Paul's prayer, how can you improve your prayers for others?

2. Why might Paul have prayed for these things and not for other things?

3. Compare this prayer of the apostle Paul with Phil 1:9-11 and Col 1:9-11. How do they differ? How are they the same? Why is Paul praying these things?

4. Do you tend to pray for your self and family or also for others? How often do you pray for others?

5. Integrate praying for "a spirit of wisdom" and "revelation in the knowledge of Him" when praying for others this week! Keep a record.

**BOOK OF EPHESIANS: BIBLE STUDIES**
*Living in the Heavenlies*

# Ephesians 1:18-23
## PENETRATING PRAYERS

Paul's prayers for the Ephesians teach us not only the importance of praying but demonstrate how to intercede for the faith of the saints around us.

➡ Share one answer of prayer that meant a lot to you.

## Basic Study Questions on Ephesians 1:18-23

> 18 I pray that the eyes of your heart may be enlightened, so that you may know what is the hope of His calling, what are the riches of the glory of His inheritance in the saints, 19 and what is the surpassing greatness of His power toward us who believe. These are in accordance with the working of the strength of His might 20 which He brought about in Christ, when He raised Him from the dead, and seated Him at His right hand in the heavenly places, 21 far above all rule and authority and power and dominion, and every name that is named, not only in this age, but also in the one to come. 22 And He put all things in subjection under His feet, and gave Him as head over all things to the church, 23 which is His body, the fulness of Him who fills all in all. (Eph 1:18-23)

1. What do you normally ask God for during the week? Answer the question and then read Ephesians 1:18-23 through. Pay close attention to what Paul the Apostle asks of the Lord.

2. In verse 18, Paul seeks for their enlightenment. What is enlightenment? What is a physical example of this?

3. List the areas that Paul prays that they would be enlightened (see verses 18-19)?

4. What is the "hope of His calling" (1:18)? What might that hope include? Do all Christians have a calling? Explain.

5. Notice the phrase "surpassing greatness of His power" in verse 19. The word 'power' already means extra strength. 'Surpassing' and 'greatness' are two other strongly descriptive words. What power is Paul talking about? What does it practically mean?

6. What does the last part of verse 19, "These are in accordance with the working of the strength of His might" refer to?

7. Fill in the blanks. Jesus Christ was _____ and _____ at God's right hand (20). How do these things demonstrate God's power?

Ephesians 1:18-23 Penetrating Prayers

8. What might "heavenly places" refer to here (1:20)?

9. Fill in the blank: Christ's rule is _____ above all rule. List the six things Paul lists that Christ's authority towers over (1:21).

10. What are a few areas that you struggle with? How can you apply God's power in these aspects to your life?

11. Who is the 'He' of verse 22? Go back in the verses until you can find the actual noun this pronoun refers to. Write it down here.

12. Verse 22 adds two other spheres that Christ has authority over. What areas are they? How do they differ?

13. What do people think the church is? How do you personally define or describe the church? How does Paul describe the church in verse 23? How is it different or the same?

14. Paul asks for many special things. What things can we learn from his prayer life for believers? Name at least one way you could improve your prayers and then pray, seeking God for these things.

# Advanced Study Questions For Ephesians 1:18-23

1. List the different parts or functions of prayer. What aspect of prayer is being demonstrated here? Write down the last five requests you made of the Lord.

2. By 'glory of His inheritance in the saints' (1:18), does Paul mean that the saints are Jesus' inheritance? Explain.

3. Verse 19 talks a lot about power. What is this power here? How does this power practically apply to a Christian's life? Be specific with at least two examples.

4. Verses 19-20 focus on God's power in Christ. Starting in verse 21, Paul identifies what establishes the great authority of Jesus Christ. Explain the relationship between power and authority. Can one have authority without power or power without authority? Christ has both.

5. Provide at least three definitions or descriptions of the church. Do they differ from Paul's description? Study the original Greek word for church, ecclesia, and include this in your comparison. The last phrase, "His body, the fulness of Him who fills all in all" is a bit mystical. What does it mean or imply? Give an instance on how this is practically worked out in your church.

6. Our prayers reveal our faith and what is important to us. Review this passage and identify what Paul asked for and talked about in his prayer.

Examine this against how you have been praying. Note any differences and mark two areas for improvement.

**BOOK OF EPHESIANS: BIBLE STUDIES**

*Living in the Heavenlies*

# Ephesians 2:1-3
## THE NEED FOR GRACE

Normally we recoil from difficult areas of life, but here we see Paul identifying and pointing out the horribly--gnarled root that lies at the core of the world's problems.

- Did you ever share an experience with the dark, satanic powers of the spirit world? If so, please share.

## Basic Study Questions on Ephesians 2:1-3

> ¹ And you were dead in your trespasses and sins, ² in which you formerly walked according to the course of this world, according to the prince of the power of the air, of the spirit that is now working in the sons of disobedience. ³ Among them we too all formerly lived in the lusts of our flesh, indulging the desires of the flesh and of the mind, and were by nature children of wrath, even as the rest. (Eph 2:1-3)

1. Read the last paragraph of Ephesians 1 and then contrast it with what is written here in Ephesians 2:1-3?

2. How are human beings described in Ephesians 2:1?

3. What differentiates 'trespass' and 'sin' from each other (2:1)? What is Paul trying to include here?

4. Does Paul here refer to being physically or spiritually dead (2:1)? What does being 'dead' mean?

5. How does Paul describe our past lives in Ephesians 2:2? What does this mean?

6. Who is he referring to here (2:2)? Why does he say 'formerly'?

7. From your own experience, describe five characteristics of the dark spiritual world.

8. Who is the "prince of the power of the air" (2:2)? Use other scriptures to help define who this one might be.

9. Do people believe the world is controlled by Satan? How would things differ if they did?

Ephesians 2:1-3 The Need for Grace                                    43

10. How does the 'spirit' of the prince of the power of the air work in people's lives (2:2)? Who exactly does the evil one influence and do his evil work through?

11. Read Ephesians 2:3. Who is he describing? What does he say about them?

12. Are Christians holier than non-believers (2:3)? What brings you to that conclusion?

13. Are God's people chosen (1:4) because of their inherent goodness? Why not? Use this verse (2:3) to prove your answer.

14. Who does this verse say God's wrath (great anger) is upon (2:3)? Why? What about 'good' people? Again, use this verse to answer this question.

15. Name three kinds of lusts (sinful desires) (2:3). How do lusts operate in an unbeliever? Do they work any differently for a believer?

16. Name two kinds of sinful desires mentioned in Ephesians 2:3? How do they differ?

17. Name at least one way this passage helps you.

## Advanced Study Questions For Ephesians 2:1-3

1. The implications of being spiritually 'dead' (2:1) are great. Some groups base their conclusion of man's depravity largely from this idea, that is, man is unable to do any good to merit salvation. God does not see any good in us and therefore chooses us apart from our good works. Can this conclusion be supported by 2:1-3? Explain.

2. Many people believe man is not that bad. These verses speak quite the opposite. Reflect on why people can arrive at the conclusion that man is inherently good. List some biblical statements asserting man is unable and unwilling to please God.

3. In verse 3, Paul is quite clear about man's drive, "lusts of our flesh, indulging the desires of the flesh and of the mind." Explain the idea of sin as described here. How does sin, the result of our lusts, relate to our fleshly desires? When do sinful desires become sin?

**BOOK OF EPHESIANS: BIBLE STUDIES**

*Living in the Heavenlies*

# Ephesians 2:4-7
## GOD'S GREAT MERCY

Did you ever need to take a second look at something astonishing? This is one of those scenes that warrants close investigation–observing God's rich mercy.

➡ What is the lowest and highest places you have visited on the earth (not including while in flight)? Where and when?

## Basic Study Questions on Ephesians 2:4-7

> ⁴ But God, being rich in mercy, because of His great love with which He loved us, ⁵ even when we were dead in our transgressions, made us alive together with Christ (by grace you have been saved), ⁶ and raised us up with Him, and seated us with Him in the heavenly places, in Christ Jesus, ⁷ in order that in the ages to come He might show the surpassing riches of His grace in kindness toward us in Christ Jesus. (Eph 2:4-7)

1. What word does Ephesians 2:4 start with? What is being contrasted here?

2. Let's use Ephesians 1 to review why God is described as being "rich in mercy" (2:1). Name five aspects of redemption from 1:3-14 where God's people receive great benefit from God. Include the verse number.

3. List three things that God does for or to His people here in Ephesians 2:4-6? (Hint: look for the verbs.)

4. What is the reason Paul gives for all the great things that God has done for us (Eph 2:4)?

5. Who does he say this love is reserved for (2:4)? Is it not for all? Explain.

6. From which state did God save us (Eph 2:5; also refer to 2:1-3)?

7. By _____ you have been _____ (2:5). Fill in the blanks.

8. What is meant in verse 5 by "made us alive together with Christ"?

9. Identify at least three other passages in the Bible that refer to the new spiritual life that God has given to us.

Ephesians 2:4-7 God's Great Mercy

10. What does Paul mean by "raised us up with Christ" (Eph 2:6)?

11. What does it mean that God "seated us with Him in the heavenly places, in Christ Jesus"? What is the difference between made alive, raised and seated?

12. What is meant by "the heavenly places" (2:6)? ('Heavenly places' is only one word in the Greek: 'heavenlies'.)

13. Why has God accomplished these three main actions <u>in Christ</u> (2:7)?

14. In verse 7 why does Paul state that God has been so magnanimous toward these individuals (think back to 2:1-4)?

15. What difference does our spiritual life make to us today? How do these truths clarify our understanding?

16. What bearing do these truths have on your prayer life?

# Advanced Study Questions For Ephesians 2:4-7

1. Reflect on what it means for Christ to live in you. Why, for example, do we face such spiritual dullness at times? Is there anything we can do to heighten our appreciation to God?

2. Why do some professing Christians seem spiritual dead? How do you resolve spiritual apathy since all Christian believers are "raised ... up with Christ"? Explain.

3. "Seated us with Him in the heavenly places" is a powerful statement. Where else is it used in Ephesians? Explain it in more detail; put it in your words. How can this affect our perspective of what's important? Why does Paul continue to return to this idea?

**BOOK OF EPHESIANS: BIBLE STUDIES**
*Living in the Heavenlies*

# Ephesians 2:8-10
## GOD'S AWESOME PLAN FOR YOU

Be careful! Professing believers often become confused about significant aspects of their Christian lives. Carefully compare these verses with some of the key beliefs of your faith and hope for eternal life.

➡ What is one thing–a grade, job, possession, spiritual achievement, etc.,– that you worked hard to get? Did you ever get it? Explain.

## Basic Study Questions on Ephesians 2:8-10

> 8 For by grace you have been saved through faith; and that not of yourselves, it is the gift of God; 9 not as a result of works, that no one should boast. 10 For we are His workmanship, created in Christ Jesus for good works, which God prepared beforehand, that we should walk in them. (Eph 2:8-10)

1. What word does verse 8 and 10 begin with? Why is it that Paul uses this word in these places?

2. Summarize Paul's key points in Ephesians 2:1-7.

3. What does it mean that God's people have been saved "by grace" (2:8)? Define grace.

4. Paul says that we have been "saved through faith" (2:8). Faith is the means through which we are saved. Does that mean faith is our contribution to being saved? What does the rest of the verse say about that? Be specific.

5. List one or several great gifts you have received. What made them great gifts? God said this salvation is a "gift of God" (2:8). What is Paul trying to stir up in us through this description? How does the idea of a gift relate to the former question?

6. Read verse 2:9. After making clear in verse 8 that salvation is completely a free gift of God, what does Paul reiterate here? What might people misunderstand about salvation?

7. List some ways people might misunderstand how good works are incorporated into our lives. What could happen as a result of this wrong thinking? How does it relate to other religions and beliefs?

8. What danger(s) would there be in boasting that we played some part in our salvation (2:9)?

Ephesians 2:8-10 God's Awesome Plan for You    51

9. In Ephesians 2:10 believers are described as what? What does this mean?

10. When did God plan the design of our lives in Christ (2:10)?

11. God says that He "created [us] in Christ Jesus for good works" (2:10). What does that mean?

12. Is the Lord interested only in works? What is needed so that they become good? Do good works differ from person to person?

13. Some believers become disappointed thinking they cannot do much for the Lord. Is the advice "Do whatever the Lord puts before you" good or bad? Why? Is that the same meaning as, "that we should walk in them" (2:10)?

14. In the future God might ask us to do things that are uncomfortable. What mindset can we adopt that would ready us for such times? What truths from Ephesians 2:10 can we use to strengthen our resolve to accomplish all that the Lord has for our lives?

15. Reflect on your life. Have you focused on what the Lord has appointed you to do or on what you want to do? Share. What steps can you take to bring your life in line with what God wants of you?

16. Choose 2-3 good works that you will do for the Lord this week that you do not usually do. Pray about them. Ask the Lord for help so you can do them with a good attitude, pleasing to Him, and thus make the 'work' a 'good work.'

## Advanced Study Questions For Ephesians 2:8-10

1. How would you define 'saved'? Do you think people differ on the meaning of this term? Give examples of this from your own experience.

2. How is it that our faith saves us? What part does faith really play in our salvation? What do we need to believe to be saved? Is it a response or the thing that we offer up to God to gain salvation (see Romans 4:13-25)?

3. Read Ephesians 2:10. Are our physical characteristics or our life situations while growing up incorporated in the larger "workmanship" for our lives? Explain.

4. Assuming the answer for the prior question is 'yes', can God make a mistake on the design of our physical bodies, sex, height, etc.? What about our situation in which He had us enter the earth: our family background, time period, wealth or poverty, type of home, etc.? Why do so many people question whether God made the best decision regarding their own lives?

5. What has God prepared beforehand (Eph 2:10)? What implication does this have on our life purpose? Are we accountable? How so? How are we to know what we are to do?

**BOOK OF EPHESIANS: BIBLE STUDIES**
*Living in the Heavenlies*

# Ephesians 2:11-18
## HE HIMSELF IS OUR PEACE

It's easy to become stressed out not only with events we don't have control over, but even more so, people. We need to grasp the peace of God that He offers us in the midst of our trials.

➡ Have you ever faced racial, cultural prejudice? Please explain.

## Basic Study Questions on Ephesians 2:11-13

> 11 Therefore remember, that formerly you, the Gentiles in the flesh, who are called "Uncircumcision" by the so-called "Circumcision," which is performed in the flesh by human hands-- 12 remember that you were at that time separate from Christ, excluded from the commonwealth of Israel, and strangers to the covenants of promise, having no hope and without God in the world. 13 But now in Christ Jesus you who formerly were far off have been brought near by the blood of Christ. (Eph 2:11-13)

1. Suggest how the "therefore" in verse 11 serves to connect these verses with 2:1-10.

2. Define what "Gentiles" means (2:11). Are you a Gentile or not?

3. Who are the uncircumcision? The circumcision (2:11)?

4. Record the five things Paul states about the Gentiles in verse 12.

    - 
    - 
    - 
    - 
    - 

5. Think of some individuals you know who have "no hope". Pray for them now.

6. What contrast is being made between verse 12 and verse 13?

7. How does the "blood of Christ" bring the Gentiles near to God (2:13)?

8. Were the Jews far off too (2:13)? Explain.

## Basic Study Questions For Ephesians 2:14-18

> ¹⁴ For He Himself is our peace, who made both groups into one, and broke down the barrier of the dividing wall, ¹⁵ by abolishing in His flesh the enmity, which is the Law of commandments contained in ordinances, that in Himself He might make the two into one new man, thus establishing peace, ¹⁶ and might reconcile them both in one body to God through the cross, by it having put to death the enmity. ¹⁷ AND HE CAME AND PREACHED PEACE TO YOU WHO WERE FAR AWAY, AND PEACE TO THOSE WHO WERE NEAR; ¹⁸ for through Him we both have our access in one Spirit to the Father. (Eph 2:14-18)

9. Jesus is our peace. How did the Lord in verse 14 cause Gentiles to be at peace with the Jews?

10. What does Paul say the enmity is in verse 15?

11. Continuing on in verse 15, he states that he brought the two groups into one man. What does this "one man" mean or refer to? Why does Paul use this expression?

12. These verses not only speak of peace among Gentile believers, but between Gentiles and Jews. Have you ever sensed that tension? Why does the blood of Christ mitigate this tension?

13. In verse 16 who are the "both" that are reconciled to God?

14. What special privilege is gained through faith in Jesus Christ (2:18)?

15. In verse 18 how many persons of the trinity are mentioned? How do they cooperate in the work of salvation?

16. Do these verses promise peace between other believers? Why don't believers often live this out?

17. What are three special ways we could more effectively live out this peace? How might such an attempt go wrong? Explain.

## Advanced Study Questions For Ephesians 2:11-18

1. What does Paul compare physical circumcision "performed in the flesh by human hands" with? Again, contrast this with God's work in the prior verses.

2. Provide three historical facts that shaped "the commonwealth of Israel".

3. Notice the apostle states "covenants of promise". What does he mean by this? The Ten Commandments or something else? Please list two of these covenants.

4. Paul speaks about the blood of Christ bringing them to the Lord. What other scriptures go into further detail? Share and explain at least two passages.

5. In verse 15, Paul says the enmity is the Law of commandments contained in ordinances. Why is this the enmity? What does it mean?

6. What is the trinity? Would you say that verse 19 proves the trinity? Why or why not?

**BOOK OF EPHESIANS: BIBLE STUDIES**

*Living in the Heavenlies*

# Ephesians 2:19-22
## NO LONGER STRANGERS

The apostle is ecstatic at the amazing grace of God seen through Christ being sent into the world. In this short passage, he speaks of four special ways God's people are uniquely blessed.

➡ What do you think about the church? Use one image to describe your thoughts.

## Basic Study Questions on Ephesians 2:19-22

> 19 So then you are no longer strangers and aliens, but you are fellow citizens with the saints, and are of God's household, 20 having been built upon the foundation of the apostles and prophets, Christ Jesus Himself being the corner stone, 21 in whom the whole building, being fitted together is growing into a holy temple in the Lord; 22 in whom you also are being built together into a dwelling of God in the Spirit. (Eph 2:19-22)

1. What is Paul referring to when he says, "So then you are no longer strangers and aliens" (2:19)? Refer to preceding verses as needed.

2. Paul will make a stark contrast between strangers and aliens (2:19) and other descriptions throughout this book. But first let's explore these terms further–name at least four characteristics of a stranger or alien.

3. The first description is "fellow citizens" (2:19). Who is he speaking to? What does this description mean? What does the added phrase "with the saints" emphasize?

4. How does this description differ from the description of strangers and aliens?

5. The next description is regarding God's household (2:19). Who is included in God's household? Explain how a person can become part of God's family?

6. What does it mean to be of God's household? How does being in God's family differ from the experience of strangers and aliens?

7. The word 'household' has a more intimate, relational feel compared to the building metaphor Paul uses in 2:20 where the term "foundation" is found. What parts of the foundation does Paul mention? Why does he emphasize them?

8. What is a cornerstone (2:20)? Do some digging into construction techniques of that day. What does it mean for Jesus to be the cornerstone?

9. Paul slowly starts transitioning to the third description of God's people in Ephesians 2:21. What is it? How does this differ from prior ones (God's household or family)?

10. Notice how Paul says the whole building … is growing (3:21). What is unusual about this? Why might Paul refer to a building in this way? (Note that 'the whole building' can also be translated every or each building.)

11. What does the word 'whole' refer to here (2:21)? How can this concept help us better appreciate those who are different from us?

12. At the end of verse 21 Paul starts using the fourth description. What is it? What is the difference between this and the former description (whole building)?

13. What does the final phrase "fitted together" refer to (2:21)? Who does the fitting? What is being fitted? What might this practically mean for our lives and churches?

14. The word for temple here refers specifically to the holy inner sanctuary where God dwelt. Read 1 Corinthians 3:16. How might this shape our perspective of the church?

15. How does this description of the temple differ from being a stranger or alien?

16. Read verses 21-22 again. Although Ephesians 2:22 might be thought of as a fifth description, it seems better to view it as summarizing the preceding verse by describing what Paul meant by a holy temple in the Lord. What can we further understand of the holy temple by verse 22?

17. Notice how he points out that God lives in His people through the Holy Spirit (2:22). What or who is the Holy Spirit? Is the Holy Spirit an 'it' (like a power) or a person (see Ephesians 4:30)?

18. Let's summarize what we have learned in this study. What are the four descriptions of God's people in Ephesians 2:19-22? How does each differ from being a stranger and alien? Share what description means most to you and why.

# Advanced Study Questions For Ephesians 2:19-22

1. Considering these four descriptions of the church, how well would you say that the church reflects these characteristics in your experience? In your diagnosis, list the strong points (where it possesses these qualities) and weak points (where it lacks these characteristics).

2. What does the greater context of chapter two have to do with Paul's use of the phrase "whole building" in verse 21? Explain its importance here.

3. The word for temple is singular rather than plural. We often think of each person as a temple, rather than all being parts of a single one. Examine the text closely and determine what is being said. How has the individualism of the West (seen elsewhere too) hurt our lives and churches? Think of several ways.

4. How can we foster more loving cooperation with each other? More fellowship? We seem to be so busy and distracted.

5. Where has the Holy Spirit so far been mentioned in the Book of Ephesians? List the theological understanding of the Holy Spirit that we gain from just these uses.

**BOOK OF EPHESIANS: BIBLE STUDIES**
Living in the Heavenlies

# Ephesians 3:1-10
## THE PURPOSE OF THE GOSPEL

Believers tend to have a very low view of their salvation. They think God was somehow obligated to save them when instead we find, as in this passage, that they are part of an incredibly glorious eternal plan.

➡ Share about some special trip or place to which you were invited.

## Basic Study Questions on Ephesians 3:1-10

¹ For this reason I, Paul, the prisoner of Christ Jesus for the sake of you Gentiles--² if indeed you have heard of the stewardship of God's grace which was given to me for you; ³ that by revelation there was made known to me the mystery, as I wrote before in brief. ⁴ And by referring to this, when you read you can understand my insight into the mystery of Christ, ⁵ which in other generations was not made known to the sons of men, as it has now been revealed to His holy apostles and prophets in the Spirit; ⁶ to be specific, that the Gentiles are fellow heirs and fellow members of the body, and fellow partakers of the promise in Christ Jesus through the gospel, ⁷ of which I was made a minister, according to the gift of God's grace which was given to me according to the working of His power. ⁸ To me, the very least of all saints, this grace was given, to

preach to the Gentiles the unfathomable riches of Christ, 9 and to bring to light what is the administration of the mystery which for ages has been hidden in God, who created all things; 10 in order that the manifold wisdom of God might now be made known through the church to the rulers and the authorities in the heavenly places. (Eph 3:1-10)

1. What do the words "for this reason" in Ephesians 3:1 refer to? Are chapters 1-2 the "cause" and chapter 3 the "effect"? Explain.

2. Who or what does Paul primarily write about in Ephesians 3:1-10? Does this seem to be typical of Paul's writing? (Does he do this elsewhere? If so, why?)

3. Where was Paul when he wrote this letter to the Ephesians (3:1; also 6:20)? How did he get to where he was? When did this happen? (See chart or Bible dictionary for assistance.)

4. What is a stewardship (3:2)? What is Paul a steward of?

5. From where did Paul receive this stewardship (3:2-3)? Paul uses the word 'revelation' in Ephesians 3:3. What is a revelation?

Ephesians 3:1-10 The Purpose of the Gospel

6. What did the apostle say happened in this revelation (3:3)? How does he further clarify this in verse 6?

7. Paul explains what a mystery is in verses 4-5. Explain Paul's idea of the word "mystery" used here.

8. Identify the three benefits non-Jewish believers have because of Christ in verse 6. Explain what each of them mean.

9. How does Paul explain the extra power to carry out this ministry (3:7)? Why is this important?

10. In verse 8 Paul continues to focus on himself. Notice the language "to me" and "the very least of all saints". Read one of the three testimonies of Paul's salvation in the Book of Acts (Acts 9, 22, 26) and explain in what sense is he one of the "very least of all saints". Do you think it is true?

11. What does Paul mean by "the unfathomable riches of Christ" in verse 8? Refer to Ephesians chapters 1-2 as necessary. Does his often used word "grace" refer to the same thing? Explain.

12. How does Paul summarize his calling in verse 9? Write it out in your own words.

13. Look in verse 10 to find out why God had called Paul to proclaim this message to the Gentiles? Explain verse 10. Who might the rulers and authorities be?

14. Do you often think about grace when thinking about your own life? How so? Why is it important for Paul and ourselves to do so?

15. One of the purposes of the church is to share the Gospel of Jesus Christ. As part of the church we are called to make what was formerly hidden known. Explain how God might want to use you to share the gospel?

# Advanced Study Questions For Ephesians 3:1-10

1. How many times did Paul use the word 'mystery' in Ephesians? Why was it so important to him?

2. The Christian faith is built on revelation, things revealed from God. Besides the Apostle Paul, state a few incidents where either Jesus or the other apostles had revelations from heaven. Can people still have visions or revelations today? Why or why not? How should we test them (1 Th 5:19-21)?

3. Discuss how reliable you think Jesus' words and the scriptures are. Where might you have doubts or would appreciate further insight into the reliability of the Gospel?

Ephesians 3:1-10 The Purpose of the Gospel

4. Why do we often find ourselves not that excited about Christ? What is wrong with our understanding? Why are we more enamored with entertainment and technology?

5. Verse 10 tells us that God uses the church to make known the Lord's manifold wisdom to those in heaven. Evidently, they are watching us here on earth (Hebrews 12:1). Did you ever think about being God's showpiece? Are you conscious of this each day? Why or why not? How could you better apply this to your life so that you can more carefully show off His glory and wisdom?

**BOOK OF EPHESIANS: BIBLE STUDIES**
Living in the Heavenlies

# Ephesians 3:11-19
## GOD'S GREATER PURPOSES

Make room for these precious truths! What the apostle shares with us here about the glorious purposes of God will astonish every believer.

➡ What makes a person rich? Why so?

## Basic Study Questions on Ephesians 3:11-19

> 11 This was in accordance with the eternal purpose which He carried out in Christ Jesus our Lord, 12 in whom we have boldness and confident access through faith in Him. 13 Therefore I ask you not to lose heart at my tribulations on your behalf, for they are your glory. 14 For this reason, I bow my knees before the Father, 15 from whom every family in heaven and on earth derives its name, 16 that He would grant you, according to the riches of His glory, to be strengthened with power through His Spirit in the inner man; 17 so that Christ may dwell in your hearts through faith; and that you, being rooted and grounded in love, 18 may be able to comprehend with all the saints what is the breadth and length and height and depth, 19 and to know the love of Christ which surpasses knowledge, that you may be filled up to all the fulness of God. (Eph 3:11-19)

1. Read Ephesians 3:8-10. What does the "this" in verse 11 refer to?

2. Verse 11 speaks of an "eternal purpose". What does this mean? Do you think it changes?

3. How does faith in Christ increase our "boldness and confident access" (3:12)?

4. Paul again speaks of "through" faith rather than through works (3:12). What does it mean? Review the previous sections and note where else in Ephesians Paul has spoken about faith in Christ.

5. Rephrase verse 13 in your own words. Why might have Paul said this?

6. Starting in verse 14, Paul starts one of His famous prayers. To whom does He address His prayer (14)? Why do many people pray to Jesus? Should they?

7. What are the implications of verse 15?

8. What does Paul pray for believers in verse 16? What does it mean? Have you ever prayed in this way? Explain.

9. What does he pray for in verse 17? Explain its meaning in your own words.

10. What does he pray for in verses 18 and 19? Explain its meaning.

11. How is that similar or dissimilar to how you pray for yourself and others?

12. How is your personal prayer life? From the way your church prays, would you say that your church believes in the importance of prayer?

13. What is the Lord and Paul's ultimate purpose in our lives (3:19)? Share an example of how God's love has overwhelmed your soul.

## Advanced Study Questions For Ephesians 3:11-19

1. What does it mean that every family in heaven and earth has derived their name from God (15)? There are two parts to this question:

    - Does heaven and earth refer to all life, spiritual and physical or just generally all people, those that now live and those who have lived?

    - What is your name? Is this the same name given to you by God? What does this God-given name mean?

2. Define the inner man (3:16). Did you ever think of how it can grow?

3. Paul states that we have bold confidence and access through faith. Note his prayer and observe his beliefs.

4. How does comprehending Christ's love surpass knowledge (3:18-19)?

5. By the last phrase in verse 19 evidently Paul has a certain picture of the church in mind as he discusses being "filled up". What image might this be? How does comprehending Christ's love contribute to being filled up?

> **BOOK OF EPHESIANS: BIBLE STUDIES**
> Living in the Heavenlies

# Ephesians 3:20-21
## EXTRAORDINARY GLORY

Doxologies are compact praises highlighting one or more special aspect of God's glorious person and work. These two slim verses drive us right to His throne.

➡ Name all the superheroes that you can. Why are they so popular?

## Basic Study Questions on Ephesians 3:20-21

> [20] Now to him who is able to do far more abundantly than all that we ask or think, according to the power at work within us, [21] to him be glory in the church and in Christ Jesus throughout all generations, forever and ever. Amen. (Eph 3:20-21 ESB)

1. Ephesians 3:20-21 is part of a longer prayer that begins in 3:14. Read the whole text aloud. Although this is one prayer, it has two parts. How do the two parts of the prayer (14-19) and (20-21) differ?

2. Ephesians 3:14-19 is an intercessory prayer. Circle the times the word 'you' is used. When is the last time you prayed for someone else? What did you ask God to do?

3. Ephesians 3:20-21 is quite different from the previous prayer. How would you describe this kind of prayer? Have you ever prayed this way before. Why or why not?

4. What set of two words are repeated in these two verses (once in 3:20 and once in 3:21)?

5. The word 'power' had been used in Ephesians five times up this point describing God's greatness. Find them and read them aloud. (The word "is able to" comes from the same root word for power but this cannot be seen in the English - "who has power to").

6. This Greek word for 'power' is *dunamis* (3:20). Can you think of any English words that have come from this Greek word relating to power?

7. Where have you seen the greatest works of power? Share and explain.

8. Explain words Paul uses to describe this power in Ephesians 3:20?

9. Where is this power said to be actively at work (3:20)? What does this practically mean?

# Ephesians 3:20-21 Extraordinary Glory

10. Let us move on and look at Ephesians 3:21. What does it say should go "to Him" (God)? What does this word mean?

11. Share one of the most glorious things you have ever seen.

12. How are the words power and glory related?

13. What are the two places that God is said to reveal His glory (3:21)?

14. Give one or two ways God's glory is shown in Jesus Christ (3:21).

15. What is the church? (The Greek word *ekklesia* literally means 'congregation' or 'assembly').

16. Give one or two ways God's glory is shown in the church (3:21).

17. Do you desire that God would be glorified through your life, family and church? Please share.

# Advanced Study Questions For Ephesians 3:20-21

1. It is normal for each Christian to both experience God's power and His glory in their lives. Have you? Pray that God would show more of His glory through your life?

2. Why would life be so much more grand if Jesus accompanied us wherever we went? How might He, in those cases, have an impact on those around you? These verses teach us that the Lord desires to live out His life through our lives (Mat 28:20). Think of one specific place you would like to see more of Jesus' power demonstrated in your life for the sake of others. Pray this through.

3. We are to live for God's praise. Write down the major things you are doing in your life through the day. Ask yourself:
   (1) Are you doing these things for God's glory?
   (2) How can you more clearly do these things for His glory.

4. Have you ever stolen God's glory? If so, name a time (and confess it if you have).

**BOOK OF EPHESIANS: BIBLE STUDIES**

*Living in the Heavenlies*

# Ephesians 4:1-3
## PRESERVING THE UNITY

Rudeness, arrogance and violence of all sorts have decimated marriages, churches and individuals. In this passage the Lord opens the door to a much better way of life.

➡ What personal character quality do you cherish most in others? Why?

## Basic Study Questions on Ephesians 4:1-3

> ¹ I, therefore, the prisoner of the Lord, entreat you to walk in a manner worthy of the calling with which you have been called, ² with all humility and gentleness, with patience, showing forbearance to one another in love, ³ being diligent to preserve the unity of the Spirit in the bond of peace. (Eph 4:1-3)

1. Read Ephesians 4:1-3. Discuss whether your church and Christians you know of are typified by what Paul says here in these first three verses. Discuss.

2. Look at the larger context for verses 4:1-3. Note how the word "therefore" {NASB} or "then" {NIV} connects this section with the former. How is what's said here connected with the former verses?

3. How does the Apostle Paul describe himself in 4:1? Why might he have said this?

4. What is the "calling" that he refers to in verse 1? Do we have the same calling?

5. Verses 2-3 describe the "manner" in which we should walk. Write down the five character traits listed for the Christian's life. Define and differentiate each of these terms (4:2-3).

    - 

    - 

    - 

    - 

    - 

6. Which trait do you have the most challenge with?

Ephesians 4:1-3 Preserving the Unity

7. What does the "unity of the Spirit" mean (4:3)?

8. What does the use of the word "preserve" (NIV - "keep") imply about this unity of the Spirit (4:3)?

9. Why does Paul encourage hem to be "diligent" to encourage them to keep this unity (4:3)?

10. What does the 'bond' of peace refer to (4:3)? (Note: bond here means 'glue.')

11. What do you find most difficult in "preserving the unity of the Spirit" (4:3)?

12. What challenges does your church have in preserving this unity?

# Advanced Study Questions For Ephesians 4:1-3

1. Our world is so brash and forceful. Does Paul's command to act humbly and gentle really make sense? Explain.

2. If two friends had a disagreement, what three or four steps could you take to help preserve the Spirit of unity?

3. Share one situation where you want to see God's unity. Pray for one another.

**BOOK OF EPHESIANS: BIBLE STUDIES**
*Living in the Heavenlies*

# Ephesians 4:4-10
## UNITY AND HARMONY

The unity of God's people, the church, is not some nice fairy tale but an accurate statement of truth in which we are to put our trust and full devotion. The evil one, knowing this, will attempt to twist our thinking.

➡ Paul in Ephesians 4:4-6 states the reason that God's people ought to act as one people. If someone asked you why God's people ought to be unified, what would you say?

## Basic Study Questions on Ephesians 4:4-6

> ⁴ There is one body and one Spirit, just as also you were called in one hope of your calling; ⁵ one Lord, one faith, one baptism, ⁶ one God and Father of all who is over all and through all and in all. (Eph 4:4-6)

1. How many times does Paul state the word 'one' in Ephesians 4:4-6? Find them. What is significant about the number of times? (Refer to Rev 1:16,20.)

2. Do you think the word "Spirit" in verse 4 refers to the Holy Spirit? Why or why not? Describe what you know about the Holy Spirit.

3. 'Calling' is a strong word that Paul used several times at the beginning of the Book of Ephesians. Glance through Ephesians 1:1-4. Who is called? Why so? What are they called to? Does it only refer to those called to full-time ministry?

4. Do you think of yourself as only having one Lord (4:5)? What does it mean? What does it practically mean to have only one Lord?

5. Does "one baptism" refer to water baptism (4:5)? Why or why not?

6. Verse 6 speaks about "one God and Father of all." What does this mean? Do you think this 'Father' concept is for everybody or exclusively the people of God? Why?

7. Read verses 4-6 again. What might you say to someone who says it's okay to have different religions as long as we worship the same God?

8. In Ephesians 4:6, Paul describes God's involvement in the world in three ways. Name them and try to differentiate one from the other.

- 
- 
-

# Basic Study Questions on Ephesians 4:7-10

The apostle uses the following verses to prove the unique identity of the body of Christ from the Old Testament by showing how the people of God became unified in Christ.

> 7 But to each one of us grace was given according to the measure of Christ's gift. 8 Therefore it says, "WHEN HE ASCENDED ON HIGH, HE LED CAPTIVE A HOST OF CAPTIVES, AND HE GAVE GIFTS TO MEN." 9 (Now this expression, "He ascended," what does it mean except that He also had descended into the lower parts of the earth? 10 He who descended is Himself also He who ascended far above all the heavens, that He might fill all things.) (Eph 4:7-10)

9. Who is Paul speaking about in verse 7? Who is included in the "us"? What is each person given (7)?

10. What does grace generally mean (e.g., Eph 2:8)? Is it used in the same way here? Explain.

11. Focus here on verse 8 which is quoted from the Old Testament (Ps 68:18). State your understanding of the meaning of the three key thoughts (listed below). It is helpful to think of the recapture of a besieged village. (Don't go too in depth as we will do this in the next verse.)

- Who ascended?

- Who are the captives?

- What is the booty He shares with men?

12. Paul explains the integral parts of verse 8 in verses 9 and 10. Verse nine speaks about Jesus' ascension.

    - What does "ascended" mean (4:9)?

    - From where did He come up (4:9)? What might that mean?

    - Summary: The reception of gifts affirms Jesus' ascension.

13. When thinking of yourself or others being lost or unsaved, do you ever think of that situation as being held captive? Explain. How does this correspond to Ephesians 2:1-2?

14. The apostle here underscores Christ's success in His mission, which gives Him authority over all, and creates a new unique body of people. Reflect on your difficulty or delight in accepting these two truths below: (Disagreement, Difficulty or Delight)

    - Jesus is Lord over the church and my life. I am indebted to Him and will unqualifyingly obey Him.

- Jesus has integrated me with other members of the body of Christ that He rescued from the enemy. I therefore remain committed to work with them to accomplish God's greater purposes.

15. Where do all the divisions come from in the body of Christ? Should we just tolerate them? What can be done? Name one thing you can do to cause more harmony in Christ's body.

# Advanced Study Questions For Ephesians 4:4-10

1. Has Paul mentioned this "body" concept before in Ephesians? Go through the Book of Ephesians and note where the "body" concept is referred to.

2. Go through the Book of Ephesians and describe what "one faith" (4:4:5) would include.

3. Secularism claims that God is not at all involved in the operations of this world or our lives. Respond to this statement using Ephesians 4:6.

4. Paul does not use the typical Greek word used for spiritual gifts (in the plural rather than singular) in this section as in other parts of the New Testament. Examine the places that *charisma* is used in the NT and try to understand why Paul did not use that word here (Ro 11:29. 12:6; 1 Cor 12:4,9, 28, 30, 31).

5. In verse 9 Paul clarifies that Jesus descended to the "lower parts of the earth" rather than just the earth (to live among men, which would be our natural interpretation). What does this mean? (This phrase is used four times in the Bible: Eph 4:9: Isa 44:23; Eze 26:20, 32:24.)

6. How is the resurrection of Jesus Christ connected to the existence of the church?

**BOOK OF EPHESIANS: BIBLE STUDIES**
*Living in the Heavenlies*

# Ephesians 4:11-16
## GOD'S GOAL FOR THE CHURCH

The theological foundation of the church is anchored in God and His mission on Earth. As an introduction to this study, make sure that you reread Ephesians 4:1-10.

➡ Consider your general knowledge of churches. What makes a good church? What makes a bad church?

## Basic Study Questions on Ephesians 4:11-13

A) God's Work in the Church

> 11 And He gave some as apostles, and some as prophets, and some as evangelists, and some as pastors and teachers, 12 for the equipping of the saints for the work of service, to the building up of the body of Christ; 13 until we all attain to the unity of the faith, and of the knowledge of the Son of God, to a mature man, to the measure of the stature which belongs to the fulness of Christ. (Eph 4:11-13)

1. What is it that the Lord has given in verse 11? Who gives it and who does He give it to (refer to 4:8-10 as needed)?

2. Do your best to define and distinguish each of the categories listed (sometimes pastor-teacher is treated as one group). What is different or similar about each one? Who does each group primarily minister to?

3. Discuss the place for apostles in today's church. Refer to Acts 14:14. Is it possible that today a 'lesser' apostle could be a missionary or church planter working in an unreached area? Why or why not? Compare with Ephesians 2:20 and 3:5.

4. Certain Bible versions use the word "saints" in 4:12. What does this word mean? Why does Paul here use it? (Notice also 1:1)

5. Why does the Lord want to equip all the people in the church (4:12)? What are the implications of this for your life?

6. Define the "work(s) of the service" in practical terms (4:12).

7. How does teaching from instructors help people do their work of service (4:12)?

8. What is the end goal for all these "works of service"? (4:13) What do each of these three phrases found in 4:13 mean?

- 

- 

- 

9. Does your church look like this? Why or why not?

10. List two or three works of service in which God has involved you. What difference does it make that you had, or didn't have, instruction to carry them out?

# Basic Study Questions on Ephesians 4:14-16

B) Our Responsibility in the Church

The Apostle Paul first tells the people of God what God intends to do in their lives (4:11-13). Now in 4:14-16 he gives three commands to properly implement it.

> 14 As a result, we are no longer to be children, tossed here and there by waves, and carried about by every wind of doctrine, by the trickery of men, by craftiness in deceitful scheming; 15 but speaking the truth in love, we are to grow up in all aspects into Him, who is the head, even Christ, 16 from whom the whole body, being fitted and held together by that which every joint supplies, according to the proper working of each individual part, causes the growth of the body for the building up of itself in love. (Eph 4:14-16)

11. What is the first command that the apostle gives to the people of God (4:14).

12. What might be a possible reason Paul writes with the concern that we might still be acting and responding like children (4:14)?

13. What are some of the "waves"–worldly philosophies, practices and unbiblical teachings–that have kept the church from being that pristine model that God has earlier given (4:14)? Which "wave" or trend has most affected you or your church?

14. What is difficult about "speaking the truth in love" (4:15)?

15. Paul instructs believers "to <u>grow up</u> in aspects into Him, who is the head, even Christ" (4:15). What is the verb used here? Write down at least three synonyms or descriptions for this word.

16. Ephesians 4:16 gives us a beautiful picture of the church illustrated by the physical human body. Discover at least four characteristics of the church.

17. Why is it that so many Christians think of growth only as something that is necessary for young Christians? They think of belief in Christ as the end rather than the beginning.

18. Reflect on your own desire to grow. Graph your spiritual growth (up, down or steady) since you became a Christian. What factors led your growth to advance or retreat? What would you like for the future? Be specific and write down your hopes before the Lord.

19. What part do you think is most lacking in your own local church? Pray for that.

# Advanced Study Questions For Ephesians 4:11-16

1. Ephesians 4:11 lists differently gifted men with authority in the church of God as they proclaim God's Word. From this verse, is "prophet" a current calling? How does your conclusion compare to other verses, and what is maintained in the church you attend?

2. The pastor-teacher is sometimes combined into one calling rather than two so that there are only four categories. Study this. Explain why this is done and whether it should be done. Does it make a key difference?

3. How does God's provision for these ministers along with the vision of equipping God's people for service affect the structure and purpose of the church? How does the seminary model, so common today, fit into this? What percentage of church members think of themselves as 'service workers'?

4. 'Christian growth' is a vague term with many assuming it only has to do with new Christians. What are the three goals of Christian growth

mentioned in Ephesians 4:13? Evaluate at least two churches. Using these three aspects of Christian growth, share how these churches are strong or weak.

**BOOK OF EPHESIANS: BIBLE STUDIES**
Living in the Heavenlies

# Ephesians 4:17-24
## LIFE TRANSFORMATION

In these few verses the Apostle Paul records <u>four</u> digressive steps away from Him and <u>three</u> steps toward Him. Learn the needed insights to overcome sin.

➡ From your general observation what is one main reason Christians are so weak in their spiritual lives? Do you see a consistent reason for this development?

## Basic Study Questions on Ephesians 4:17-19

Four Downward Steps

> ¹⁷ This I say therefore, and affirm together with the Lord, that you walk no longer just as the Gentiles also walk, in the futility of their mind, ¹⁸ being darkened in their understanding, excluded from the life of God, because of the ignorance that is in them, because of the hardness of their heart; ¹⁹ and they, having become callous, have given themselves over to sensuality, for the practice of every kind of impurity with greediness. (Eph 4:17-19)

1. What is Paul saying in verse 17-18? State it in your own words.

2. What is the world like (4:17-18)? Is it really as Paul says? Explain.

3. Briefly list the declining spiral steps towards depravity seen in verses 17-19. Rephrase them in your own words as necessary.

4. What does it add to the meaning when he states "together with the Lord" (Eph 4:17)?

5. What are the reasons Paul gives for their sinful ways (4:18)?

6. After the darkening of the mind, Paul describes other ways that their lives will further digress from God's standards. What are they? See Ephesians 4:19.

## Basic Study Questions on Ephesians 4:20-24

### Three Upward Steps

> 20 But you did not learn Christ in this way, 21 if indeed you have heard Him and have been taught in Him, just as truth is in Jesus, 22 that, in reference to your former manner of life, you lay aside the old self, which is being corrupted in accordance with the lusts of deceit, 23 and that you be renewed in the spirit of your mind, 24 and put on the new self, which in the likeness of God has been

# Ephesians 4:17-24 Life Transformation

created in righteousness and holiness of the truth. (Eph 4:20-24)

7. List the three transforming steps that Christians should take in their lives as they pursue righteousness, holiness and truth (4:22-24)?

8. What is the first step of transformation (4:22)? Explain what it means in your own words.

9. Does the Christian life promise to renew or 'fix' the old nature (4:22)? Why?

10. Why is this step so important in handling temptation (4:22)?

11. What is the second step of transformation (4:23)? What does this mean? Is it a one-time event? Refer to Romans 12:2.

12. Can a person take the second renewal step (renewed in the spirit of your mind 4:23) without taking the first? How do steps one and two relate to each other? Explain.

13. The third step is to "put on the new self." How does Paul amplify the meaning of this (4:24)?

14. Does verse 24 mean that each believer has the new nature made in the image of God? If this is so, why do believers still sin or want what sin offers?

15. Give one or two examples of how you have personally seen these three steps of God's grace take place in your own life.

16. What step or area of Christian growth have you struggled with most? Explain your difficulty using these verses.

## Advanced Study Questions For Ephesians 4:17-24

1. How does the pattern *ignorance>hardening>sensuality>impurity* reflect itself in what the apostle has said in Romans 1:20-27?

2. How does becoming in the "likeness of God" reflect the phrase "in the image of God" in Genesis 1:27?

3. Understanding how the old and new nature work in a Christian's life largely determines how much a believer will struggle in his or her spiritual life. How would you explain, using the transformation steps above, some of the difficult questions that believers face?

- If I am a believer, why do I still have desires to sin?

- How can I overcome what are often very strong impulses to sin?

- How does this new nature work in my life? How can I implement this truth more successfully in my life?

## BOOK OF EPHESIANS: BIBLE STUDIES
*Living in the Heavenlies*

# Ephesians 4:25
## PURE LIVING (PART 1)

Starting in verse 25, Paul gives examples of how we can apply the three steps of life transformation taught in the previous section. This verse shows how to replace falsehood with the truth.

➡ Give an example of something you have lied about or how you have deceived someone.

## Basic Study Questions on Ephesians 4:25

> 25 Therefore, laying aside falsehood, SPEAK TRUTH, EACH ONE *of you*, WITH HIS NEIGHBOR, for we are members of one another (Eph 4:25).

1. What is falsehood (4:25)? Use at least three descriptions of how falsehood displays itself.

2. What does Ephesians 4:25 tell you to do with falsehood in your life? What does this mean?

3. As a review, reread Ephesians 4:24. Describe the new self. How does this description relate to the way a believer is to understand and handle falsehood and deceit?

4. Man was not always a liar. When did lying begin? What were some signs of falsehood found in Genesis 3?

5. What are you told to positively do in verse 4:25?

6. What is truth? What does it mean to "speak truth"?

7. Who is to speak truth (25)? Is anyone excluded?

8. Why do people tend to think it is okay for them to lie at times? It is right to think this way? What are some excuses used to defend their lies?

9. What are the advantages of speaking the truth?

10. What motivation does Ephesians 4:25 give us to speak the truth?

# Ephesians 4:25 Pure Living (Part 1)

11. Jesus' royal law says, "You shall love your neighbor as yourself" (James 2:8). Do you like to be lied to? Why not?

12. What harm do rumors, slander and gossip bring? Have you experienced these? Please share.

13. When we lay aside our falsehood, we often are afraid of the consequences. Name some possible consequences if you tell the truth instead of lying. Note your need to depend upon God for help to live a life of truth.

14. Share what the following verses say about falsehood and speaking the truth.
"The wicked earns deceptive wages, But he who sows righteousness gets a true reward. He who is steadfast in righteousness will attain to life, And he who pursues evil will bring about his own death. The perverse in heart are an abomination to the LORD, But the blameless in their walk are His delight. Assuredly, the evil man will not go unpunished, But the descendants of the righteous will be" delivered (Proverbs 11:18-21).

15. Make a time chart of your life. Graph out how much you use falsehood in your daily life, past, present and future. This prediction of your future is related to your commitment by His grace to obey God's Word.

16. Ephesians 4:25 tells us to "lay aside falsehood". The real way to do this, once for all, is to go to God and those you have lied to, speak the truth of what you did wrong, why it was wrong and to ask for forgiveness. Pay remuneration if needed. Is God prompting you to do this for any particular situation? (See the Advanced Study Questions below for more detail.)

## Advanced Study Questions For Ephesians 4:25

1. Is it okay to lie to children? Why or why not? Explain how parents and teachers could use God's promises to comfort children rather than lying to them. Give an example of how we lie to children (a spreading disease, dying parent, Dad losing his job).

2. Make a plan to lay aside falsehood and speak the truth. List all the unconfessed falsehoods that come to your mind in the left column. In the middle column list the people you yet need to confess your deceiving ways. In the third (last) column write the date that you have fully admitted the truth before God and man. Claim the blood of Christ over all these lies and pledge yourself before God to speak only the truth. You should experience greater moral courage and a closer walk with God.

# BOOK OF EPHESIANS: BIBLE STUDIES
Living in the Heavenlies

# Ephesians 4:26-32
## PURE LIVING (PART 2)

The old nature, as explained in the previous verses, expresses itself in many ways. We are to deny these evil expressions which Paul shares and adopt the behavior and thoughts stemming from the new nature!

➡ Why is it so hard not to be angry and stay angry?

## Basic Study Questions on Ephesians 4:26-28

> 26 BE ANGRY, AND yet DO NOT SIN; do not let the sun go down on your anger, 27 and do not give the devil an opportunity. 28 Let him who steals steal no longer; but rather let him labor, performing with his own hands what is good, in order that he may have something to share with him who has need. (Eph 4:26-28)

1. What are God's people instructed to do and not to do in verse 26?

2. Paul says first to "be angry" (4:26). Isn't anger sin? Isn't anger the source of so much evil in this world? What does he mean?

3. What are the special instructions at the tail end of verse 26? What does this practically mean? How are we to get rid of anger before we go to sleep? Please be specific.

4. In verse 27, Paul suggests that not getting rid of your anger at night gives the devil special access to our hearts and lives. How might that happen? Do you have any habits of checking your spirit before going to sleep? Explain.

5. Read verse 28. Why do people steal? Is it okay to steal (4:28)? Why do people make exceptions for stealing small things? Is this just as bad as stealing large items?

6. What kind of lifestyle does the apostle command us to take up in place of stealing (4:28)? What advantage does this have for our lives and those around us?

## Basic Study Questions On Ephesians 4:29-32

> [29] Let no unwholesome word proceed from your mouth, but only such a word as is good for edification according to the need of the moment, that it may give grace to those who hear. [30] And do not grieve the Holy Spirit of God, by whom you were sealed for the day of redemption. [31] Let all bitterness and wrath and anger and clamor and slander be put away from you, along with all malice. [32] And be kind to one another, tender-hearted, forgiving each other, just as God in Christ also has forgiven you. (Eph 4:29-32)

7. What do some people object to swearing (e.g., saying 4 letter words) (4:29)? Explain. What kind of words are included in "unwholesome" words? With what are we to replace these unwholesome words (4:29)?

8. How do unwholesome words and from words of edification differ in their effect (4:29)? Which do you prefer? Do you still use unwholesome words? If so, why?

9. Verse 30 says that we should not "grieve the Holy Spirit". What does that mean? What are some examples of what we do or say that grieves our Lord? (Note: When Jesus ascended, Jesus sent the Holy Spirit to work in our lives (John 16:1-13.)

10. When were believers "sealed" by the Holy Spirit (refer Eph 1:13)? Was it a one time event? How is it different from being filled with the Spirit (Eph 5:18)?

11. List the five things Paul says we should stop doing in verse 31. How do they differ from each other? Use a dictionary as needed.

12. With what are we to replace mean attitudes and actions (4:32)? For example, how is bitterness opposite to what we read in verse 32?

13. How are we to forgive each other (4:32)? List five characteristics of this type of forgiveness?

14. Do you quickly forgive others? Should we forgive others even if they do not apologize? What does verse 32 say regarding this?

## Advanced Study Questions For Ephesians 4:26-32

1. How does Jesus reveal and condemn anger's source in the Sermon on the Mount (Mat 5:21-25)? Explain.

2. With which of the Ten Commandments is stealing connected (Exodus 20:1-17)? Explain.

3. Verse 30 says we "were sealed for the day of redemption" by the Holy Spirit. Search for "sealed" in the Book of Revelation and note how the word is used. How is "sealed" used here in Eph 4:30 and in Eph 1:13? How does being sealed fit in with the other aspects of salvation?

4. Go through the verses for this lesson and mark one chief thing you need to stop doing and one that you need to start doing. Are they related to each other? If so, how? Pray about this and memorize the related verses.

**BOOK OF EPHESIANS: BIBLE STUDIES**

*Living in the Heavenlies*

# Ephesians 5:1-7
## PURE LIVING (PART 3)

When God works in our lives to save us, He does not merely save us from the penalty of sin but also from the power of sin. In this section Paul continues to present what our transformed lives as the children of God should look like.

➡ List three objects that once were valuable but you later threw away? Why did you get rid of them?

## Basic Study Questions on Ephesians 5:1-2

> ¹ Therefore be imitators of God, as beloved children; ² and walk in love, just as Christ also loved you, and gave Himself up for us, an offering and a sacrifice to God as a fragrant aroma. (Eph 5:1-2)

1. What word marks the beginning of chapter five? (Remember that chapters, verses and punctuation were added later to the scriptures.) Look at the previous verses at the end of Ephesians 4 and try to explain what the "therefore" at the beginning of chapter 5 is 'there for'?

2. Verse 1 says that we are to act "as beloved children." List several ways children reflect their parents.

3. What are Christians called to do in verse 1? Name at least three ways that we as Christians can imitate God.

4. Do you think it is too idealistic to think humans can be like God? Please explain. What did Paul think?

5. What else does the apostle tell us to do in verse 2? Does loving others seem like a joy or burden to you? Explain.

6. How does Paul say that are we to love others (2)?

7. What does it mean that Jesus gave Himself up for us as a sacrifice (2)? Why would this please God (i.e. fragrant aroma) and have Him offer up His Son to die for us?

8. Read verses 5:1-2 again. Why do you think Paul wrote these verses?

# Basic Study Questions on Ephesians 5:3-7

> 3 But do not let immorality or any impurity or greed even be named among you, as is proper among saints; 4 and there must be no filthiness and silly talk, or coarse jesting, which are not fitting, but rather giving of thanks. 5 For this you know with certainty, that no immoral or impure

Ephesians 5:1-7 Pure Living (Part 3)

person or covetous man, who is an idolater, has an inheritance in the kingdom of Christ and God. ⁶ Let no one deceive you with empty words, for because of these things the wrath of God comes upon the sons of disobedience. ⁷ Therefore do not be partakers with them. (Eph 5:3-7)

9. Name the three things Paul identifies in verse 3 with which we are not to be associated. Define each. What is the difference between them?

10. Find three other places the word "saints" is used in the New Testament (used 8 times in Ephesians) (5:3)? What does the word "saint" mean?

11. Among the three areas of sin listed in verse 3, which in your opinion has to the greatest degree infiltrated the church of God? Which do you personally need to fight the most? Please elaborate.

12. Explain the difference between the three ways we are admonished not to speak in verse 4.

13. What does it mean that our speech is to be characterized by "giving of thanks" (5:4)?

14. Verse 5 clearly asserts that certain people will not inherit eternal life. Who are these people? Why do you think Paul added the phrase, "For this you know with certainty" (5:5)?

15. What "empty words" does Paul seem to refer to in verse 6? How could they deceive us?

16. Read verse 6 again. What does "wrathful" mean? Is God wrathful? Isn't God a God of love (5:1)? Explain.

17. What does Paul warn us from doing in verse 7? What does that practically mean in your situation?

18. Review the teaching of this section by stating three things we are to be like and five things we are not to be like. What is one area of your life in which you need special work? Make a plan to do this.

19. Pray for the lost people around you. God's wrath is about to fall on them. Seek a way you can share the gospel with at least one of these people.

# Advanced Study Questions For Ephesians 5:1-7

1. Verse 2 speaks about Christ's death serving as a "sacrifice" for us, whereas Romans 3:24-25, He 2:17, 1 John 2:2 and 4:10 all use the

# Ephesians 5:1-7 Pure Living (Part 3)

specialized word "propitiation" instead of "sacrifice" (NASB). What is the difference between the word "propitiation" and the general word "sacrifice"?

2. What vulgar or inappropriate speech do you hear? Are there any words that you use but would not openly say in front of your pastor? Explain.

3. Can the phrase "has not an inheritance in the kingdom of Christ and God" (5) be simplified by "will not inherit eternal life" (see question 14 above)? Are they the same? Explain.

4. Verse 5 ("has not an inheritance...") shakes up some believers as they do not know how to resolve what is stated here with other parts of God's Word. Here are two other truths that this definitive statement about some professing believers must be resolved.

- God promised eternal life to those who believe, but it appears people can lose their salvation here if they do not live to certain standards stated in scripture (e.g. 1 Cor 6:9-10).

- God said that we are saved by grace through faith (Eph 2:8-9) so how is it that salvation appears to depend upon our good works?

Both conclusions are wrong. What is the right way to resolve the problem? Remember the clear truths from Ephesians: believers have eternal life and are saved by faith, not by good works.

5. Some people say that the God of the Old Testament is a 'God of wrath' while the God of the New Testament is a 'God of love'. What is wrong with this assertion? Please relate the biblical support you have for your assessment.

**BOOK OF EPHESIANS: BIBLE STUDIES**

*Living in the Heavenlies*

# Ephesians 5:8-14
## CHILDREN OF LIGHT

The Christian is in a spiritual battle (Eph 6:11). Sometimes one teaching will be used by God to bring a needed breakthrough in our lives. At other times, another teaching might help more. The apostle here uses the powerful illustration of light that can help illuminate our minds in very dark and confusing times.

➡ Share an experience when you were in a very dark place. What do you remember feeling?

## Basic Study Questions on Ephesians 5:8-14

> 8 For you were formerly darkness, but now you are light in the Lord; walk as children of light 9 (for the fruit of the light consists in all goodness and righteousness and truth), 10 trying to learn what is pleasing to the Lord. 11 And do not participate in the unfruitful deeds of darkness, but instead even expose them; 12 for it is disgraceful even to speak of the things which are done by them in secret. 13 But all things become visible when they are exposed by the light, for everything that becomes visible is light. 14 For this reason it says, "Awake, sleeper, And arise from the dead, And Christ will shine on you" (Eph 5:8-14).

1. What does Paul mean in Ephesians 5:8 that "you were formerly darkness?" Isn't that a rather severe statement?

2. What does he mean by stating that "you are now light?" Isn't that a bit exaggerated? (5:8). Is it true for all Christians?

3. What does it mean to be "children of light" (5:8)?

4. How does the apostle describe light or its fruit in verse 9? Define each term in your own words to the best of your ability.

5. How does Ephesians 5:10 summarize our goal as God's children? How does that relate to the topic of light?

6. What does he warn against doing in verse 11? What does he say to do?

7. Does verse 12 limit what and when we should speak about some of the terrible things in this world? Is this similar to parents who teach their children, "Be quiet. We don't talk about such things."

8. What principle of light is mentioned in verse 13?

Ephesians 5:8-14 Children of Light

9. Explain how the principle of light identified in verse 13 works in a spiritual sense. Give at least three examples.

10. Where do the words from Ephesians 5:14 come from? Reference a website or book as needed.

11. Why do you think Paul quotes these words in verse 14?

12. What does he tell us to do in verse 14? What will happen if we do? Which describes you better, awake or sleeping?

13. How does one accomplish what he says to do in Ephesians 5:14? Give a practical example of how this is done.

## Advanced Study Questions For Ephesians 5:8-14

1. Make as many observations about light that you can concerning its various properties. Include both physical observations as well as principles you might have learned in a science class.

2. Read Matthew 5:14-16. How does this relate to the passage here in Ephesians 5:8-14?

3. How would you advise a Christian who feels more like darkness than light? Remember to use Paul's counsel in these verses.

4. Why is the society so dark? Do you think it is related to how well lit the church is? Explain.

5. The key for revival is in verse 14. How would you share with another Christian the relevance and urgency of this teaching?

6. Have you ever dared to step closer to God so that more of your darkness would show up? Please give an example.

**BOOK OF EPHESIANS: BIBLE STUDIES**
*Living in the Heavenlies*

# Ephesians 5:15-21
## FILLED WITH THE SPIRIT

If we really want to know God's will, then we need a heart to do it whenever He speaks, whatever He requests and with whomever He brings into our lives.

➡ Share you opinion on what it means to be filled with the Spirit of God.

## Basic Study Questions on Ephesians 5:15-17

### A) Living by the will of God

<sup>15</sup> Therefore be careful how you walk, not as unwise men, but as wise, <sup>16</sup> making the most of your time, because the days are evil. <sup>17</sup> So then do not be foolish, but understand what the will of the Lord is. (Eph 5:15-17)

1. What two kinds of people does Paul mention in verse 5:15? What is the difference between the way each of them walks or makes decisions? List at least three differences.

2. Paul in verse 15 tells us to be "careful how you walk," alluding to potential danger. Name at least three dangers you might face if you were not careful.

3. Paul says "the days are evil" (5:16). What does that mean in the larger context of chapter 5 and in the world in which you live?

4. Can a believer act foolishly (5:17)? Explain by using verse 17. The "but" in verse 17 contrasts the foolish person with the one who does the will of God. Do you agree the will of God always excludes foolishness? Explain.

5. The will of God is often questioned by us and thought as less than ideal. Pick at least one of the areas that you struggle with below and discuss it considering God's good and perfect will (Romans 12:2).

   - Why is it that a wife at times insists on something that the husband disagrees with?

   - Why is it that the child thinks anyone is right but his or her parents?

   - Why does a church member persist in thinking his way is best even when the elders dismiss the idea? Is that good?

# Basic Study Questions on Ephesians 5:18-21

## B) Being filled with the Holy Spirit

> 18 And do not get drunk with wine, for that is dissipation, but be filled with the Spirit, 19 speaking to one another in psalms and hymns and spiritual songs, singing and making melody with your heart to the Lord; 20 always giving thanks for all things in the name of our Lord Jesus Christ to God, even the Father; 21 and be subject to one another in the fear of Christ. (Eph 5:18-21)

6. Is drinking alcohol okay? What about getting drunk (5:18)? What word does Paul use to describe drunkenness? Look up its definition and describe what you know of drunkenness to support its prohibition (18).

7. How is being filled with the Spirit of God opposite to getting drunk (5:18)?

8. Is being filled with the Spirit a one-time event, or something that regularly happens (18)? Explain your answer.

9. What are the three kinds of songs Paul mentions in verse 19? (Note: Paul is probably comparing drunk people who sing when drunk with those who worship through song.) How do they differ? What songs does your church favor? Is one kind of song more spiritual than another? Explain.

10. Why do Christians place so much emphasis on music? What is its purpose (5:19)?

11. Paul uses three ways to describe the person filled with the Spirit of God. The first is worship through music, what are the other two? Check out verses 20 and 21.

12. Why is giving thanks so important (5:20)?

13. When are we to give thanks (5:20)? For what are we to give thanks?

14. Do you tend to give thanks or complain? If we use giving thanks as a measuring unit, could you say that you are filled with the Spirit of God? Explain.

15. Verse 21 instructs us to be subject to one another in the fear of Christ. What does it practically mean to be "subject to one another?"

16. What additional sense does the phrase "in the fear of Christ" bring to this admonition (5:21)?

# Ephesians 5:15-21 Filled With the Spirit

17. What are the difficulties with constantly being filled with the Spirit of God? What is your biggest challenge?

18. How is this filling with the Spirit of God related to living in the reflection or image of God (cf. Eph 5:1-2)?

## Advanced Study Questions for Ephesians 5:15-21

1. Some churches have fought and even split over the issue of what type of music and songs are to be used in worship. Why does this happen? How can this tension be alleviated?

2. What are the three expressions of being filled with the Spirit of God? (18-21)? How does this differ from what most people think of as being filled with the Spirit? Is there any misunderstanding in your church or nation about this?

3. Explain the theology of why we must give thanks "in the name of the Lord Jesus Christ to God?" (5:20) Do we need to say this every time we give thanks? Explain.

4. Some suggest that "subject to one another" means that husbands need to be subject to their wives (see verse 22)? Does this make sense? Can the one in authority be subject to the one under his authority?

**BOOK OF EPHESIANS: BIBLE STUDIES**
*Living in the Heavenlies*

# Ephesians 5:22-30
## IMPROVING ONE'S MARRIAGE

Many marriages would greatly improve through the creation of an atmosphere of peace, joy and love if husbands and wives simply took the advice given in these verses. Why don't we simply trust God more?

➡ What is one marital struggle that you have or your parents had?

## Basic Study Questions on Ephesians 5:22-24

> ²² Wives, be subject to your own husbands, as to the Lord. ²³ For the husband is the head of the wife, as Christ also is the head of the church, He Himself being the Savior of the body. ²⁴ But as the church is subject to Christ, so also the wives ought to be to their husbands in everything. (Eph 5:22-24)

1. What are wives instructed to do in verse 22? What does this practically mean?

2. Evidently, since only one command was given to wives, wives have special difficulty with subjecting themselves to their husbands. Do you find this true? If so, why do you think this is the case?

3. What additional words does Paul add to this command at the end of verse 22? What extra rationale does this add to the command for wives to be subject to their husbands?

4. Some wives will challenge anyone that tells them that they need to be subject to their husbands. How does Paul in verse 23 answer the question, "Upon what authority should wives subject themselves to their husbands?"

5. How is the husband head of the wife (5:23)? What does this practically mean? Some think this would include abusive behavior or speech. Why is this not so?

6. How did the apostle expand or clarify this subjection for the wife in verse 24? Why might that little phrase at the end be added?

7. Do you find that people in your local church have problems in subjecting themselves to the Lord? Provide some examples.

8. Are there any exceptions for this strong command? For example, are there any times the husband can stop loving his wife? What if his wife is unresponsive, left home or is going through severe mood swings?

# Basic Study Questions on Ephesians 5:25-30

> ²⁵ Husbands, love your wives, just as Christ also loved the church and gave Himself up for her; ²⁶ that He might sanctify her, having cleansed her by the washing of water with the word, ²⁷ that He might present to Himself the church in all her glory, having no spot or wrinkle or any such thing; but that she should be holy and blameless. ²⁸ So husbands ought also to love their own wives as their own bodies. He who loves his own wife loves himself; ²⁹ for no one ever hated his own flesh, but nourishes and cherishes it, just as Christ also does the church, ³⁰ because we are members of His body. (Eph 5:25-30)

9. What are husbands commanded to do in verse 25? What is the husband's love to be characterized by (5:25)? Be specific.

10. Which command do you think is harder: The one for the wives or the one for the husbands? Explain.

11. For what purpose does the Lord say He loves the church in verse 26? What does "sanctify" mean here?

12. What is the reason Paul gives in verse 27 for Christ making His people holy (sanctified)? Try to put this in your own words.

13. Verse 28 again commands the husbands to love their wives. What additional emphasis is added here and what additional meaning is given through this emphasis?

14. Paul states, he who "loves his own wife loves himself" (5:28). On what basis does he state this (see 5:29)? Why is it critical for the husbands to understand this?

15. What does Paul state in verse 30? Why is this relevant to the subject of husbands and wives?

16. Give one example of how husbands can learn to love their wives by following Jesus' example of loving His own disciples when they were not listening to Him.

17. How is a husband to deal with a wife that is not subjecting herself to him? How is a wife to subject herself to a husband whom she does not trust?

18. If married, think of the greatest challenge you have to love your spouse. Reflect on how Paul's instruction might relate to it. If not yet married, think of your parents' husband-wife relationship and note any problems or blessings from the way they respond to these truths expressed here.

# Advanced Study Questions for Ephesians 5:22-30

1. Go back to the original garden scene. Do you find any connection between Eve's original sin and wives' general difficulty in submitting to their husbands today?

2. "As to the Lord" (Eph 5:22) could have various interpretations, including the following:
   (a) In attitude: subject yourself to your husband in the same attitude you would talk to or obey the Lord Jesus.
   (b) In sphere: only be subject to your husbands in areas that the Lord would approve of. Which of these, or perhaps others, is the most accurate interpretation? Why?

3. How is the appointment of the husband as authority or head over the wife important? What happens when there is no clearly appointed head? Have you seen the results of a marriage without a clear agreement as to who was in charge? Describe.

4. How does Jesus sanctify the church with His Word (Eph 5:26)?

5. How is the husband and wife covenant like the covenant Christ has with the church? Upon what Genesis passage is the former founded? Read it aloud.

6. Do you think that marriage as described in the Bible is a man-made social construct or is it God-made? Please explain using Genesis 1-3 and other biblical support.

**BOOK OF EPHESIANS: BIBLE STUDIES**
Living in the Heavenlies

# Ephesians 5:31-33
## THE PICTURE OF MARRIAGE

Most couples have never thought of their marriage as a picture of the spiritual covenant God forms between His Son Jesus and His bride, the people of God.

➡ What do people around you believe about marriage? Does a person's view of marriage make any difference to one's marriage?

## Basic Study Questions on Ephesians 5:31-33

> 31 FOR THIS CAUSE A MAN SHALL LEAVE HIS FATHER AND MOTHER, AND SHALL CLEAVE TO HIS WIFE; AND THE TWO SHALL BECOME ONE FLESH. 32 This mystery is great; but I am speaking with reference to Christ and the church. 33 Nevertheless let each individual among you also love his own wife even as himself; and let the wife see to it that she respect her husband. (Eph 5:31-33)

1. Who created marriage? What in verse 31 proves this?

2. The world's ways always bring decay and disaster. What evidence have you seen in a couple's marriage that show they have left God, even including professing Christians?

3. What is the husband's two-pronged calling from God (5:31)? What does each practically mean?

4. Do you think that by "leav(ing) his father and mother" (5:31) refers to the parents' house or also their authority? Are these the same? Explain.

5. What is the 'great mystery' (5:32) stated at the end of verse 31? Is this more than bodily oneness? Explain.

6. Jesus used this same Old Testament quote to show how divorce is wrong and remarriage is adultery (Mark 10:8-12). How does 'oneness' illustrate that divorce is wrong? Why is remarriage adultery (if the former spouse is still living)?

7. Many people speak of intimacy in marriage. How does oneness support this thought (5:31)?

8. Marriage a picture of what (5:32)? Explain.

# Ephesians 5:31-33 The Picture of Marriage

9. What kind of intimacy is suggested by the covenant between Christ and His people (5:32)? How does that intimacy translate to marriage?

10. Why does Paul return to discussing earthly marriages rather than ending this discussion discussing spiritual union (5:33)? (See the word "nevertheless.")

11. What are the two commands that Paul reiterates in 5:33? Are they any different from what was formerly stated? Explain.

12. Do you see these two commands as bringing tension into the marriage or leading to harmony and union? Why? What do you think God's intention is?

13. Describe what a husband's love is to look like. You can go through this whole passage of Ephesians 5:31-33 to find other words to help describe or illustrate this love but remember to get practical.

14. How can a single man or even boy begin to train himself for marriage? List at least three things.

15. What is the wife called to do in Ephesians 5:33? How does the word 'respect' similar to or differ from the command to 'be subject' to her husband (5:22,24)?

16. Is submissiveness a passive or active state? How can a wife deliberately submit to her husband?

17. Are women trained to be submissive today? How are women going to be good wives if they are not trained in this way? What is a way yet-to-be wives can train themselves in this area?

18. How should a wife respond to her husband if he is not living according to God's ways? Support your answer with at least one clear scripture passage.

## Advanced Study Questions for Ephesians 5:31-33

1. Sometimes it is hard for singles to talk about marriage. Singles however are learning attitudes early on that will affect their marriage. Unfortunately, most of these attitudes are not good. What is wrong with most relationships they see in the videos they watch?

2. What biblical evidence do we have that the wife fills a very important part of a husband's life? (Hint: see Genesis 2.)

3. Marriage is to inspire us with unity, harmony and depth of friendship. This is seen at the wedding, but is it found anywhere else? Explain.

Ephesians 5:31-33 The Picture of Marriage 137

4. Four major heresies that have invaded the modern world are secularism, an independent spirit, materialism, and feminism. Define each. How has each affected Christian marriage and families? Give support for your answer. List the right perspectives that correct these four heresies.

5. Do you believe that obedience to God's Word will result in a good marriage and family, and that disobedience results in bad marriages and families? If so, then discuss what it takes to have a good marriage.

6. It is helpful for people to share how they were trained for marriage by their parents (for good or bad). People learn from their parents in two ways: by observing (1) parents and children interactions and (2) father and mother interactions.

**BOOK OF EPHESIANS: BIBLE STUDIES**
*Living in the Heavenlies*

# Ephesians 6:1-4
## FAMILY MATTERS

Our culture has no clue about how to properly parent its children. It has left the wisdom gained from the scriptures and preceding generations. This is where the basics are found!

➡ What is one thing your parents did right and one thing they did wrong?

## Basic Study Questions on Ephesians 6:1-4

> ¹ Children, obey your parents in the Lord, for this is right. ² Honor your father and mother (which is the first commandment with a promise), ³ that it may be well with you, and that you may live long on the earth. ⁴ And, fathers, do not provoke your children to anger; but bring them up in the discipline and instruction of the Lord. (Eph 6:1-4)

1. Who are children told to obey (6:1)?

2. What does "obey" mean (6:1)?

3. How should a child respond to his parent's command if he or she doesn't feel like obeying his or her parents (6:1-2)?

4. What makes a child's obedience so important – "this is right" (6:1)?

5. How is 'honor' different from 'obey' (6:1-2)?

6. For how long should a person obey and honor his parents? What other principles might apply for our older children?

7. What is the promise that is associated with the command in this section (Eph 6:2-3)?

8. How does obedience relate to having a good life and living long?

9. What are the three things fathers are told to do in Ephesians 6:4?

10. What does it mean not to "provoke your children to anger"? How might a father provoke his child? Share an incident from your life where you provoked someone or were provoked.

# Ephesians 6:1-4 Family Matters 141

11. Why might Paul address the fathers here in Ephesians 6:4 and not the mothers?

12. What does the word "discipline" mean in Ephesians 6:4? Why does the world–or even the church–neglect or even reject discipline when training children?

13. What kind of instruction is mentioned here? How can parents implement this? Again, share from your own experiences.

## Advanced Study Questions for Ephesians 6:1-4

1. Some Christian parents fear having children today, afraid they might run after the world. What would Paul the apostle say about this from these verses?

2. What would you say to parents who feel that they cannot shape their children's behavior?

3. How should a parent properly discipline and chastise his or her child?

4. What steps should a father take to prevent himself from provoking his children?

**BOOK OF EPHESIANS: BIBLE STUDIES**

*Living in the Heavenlies*

# Ephesians 6:5-9
## RESPONSIBILITIES AND OPPORTUNITIES

Is avoiding hard work a good thing? The Lord has much to say about our attitudes towards work, whether we are being paid, volunteering, at home or are in retirement.

➡ Share one attribute of a good worker.

## Basic Study Questions on Ephesians 6:5-9

> 5 Slaves, be obedient to those who are your masters according to the flesh, with fear and trembling, in the sincerity of your heart, as to Christ; 6 not by way of eyeservice, as men-pleasers, but as slaves of Christ, doing the will of God from the heart. 7 With good will render service, as to the Lord, and not to men, 8 knowing that whatever good thing each one does, this he will receive back from the Lord, whether slave or free. 9 And, masters, do the same things to them, and give up threatening, knowing that both their Master and yours is in heaven, and there is no partiality with Him. (Eph 6:5-9)

1. What are the two groups that Paul addresses in Ephesians 6:5-9?

2. What are slaves commanded to do in verse 5? What does "masters, according to the flesh" mean?

3. Why is "fear and trembling" an important part to proper service (6:5)? Is not fear something to avoid?

4. Paul commands that slaves serve their earthly masters "in the sincerity of your hearts not by way of eye service, as men-pleasers" (6:5-6). What common problem do you think Paul is trying to address concerning slaves? Do those who are not slaves have this problem? Explain.

5. Pick out three roles/jobs that you are familiar with. Describe the difference of performing these duties improperly "by way of eyeservice, as men-pleasers" and properly, "sincerely of your heart to Christ".

6. Can slaves in their low position serve God? How do we know this from verse 6?

7. What is the will of God (6:6)? What is the difference of doing God's will out of compulsion and doing it from the heart?

8. Read verse 7 then answer, "Do you think a slave is right to slack off on service to a mean master?" Please explain your answer. Is the same true if we have a mean or unkind boss?

Ephesians 6:5-9 Responsibilities and Opportunities

9. State the promise from verse 8 in your own words. How might that make a difference in the way a mistreated servant carries out his or her work?

10. In verse 9 he addresses the believing masters. What do you think he means by "do the same things to them?"

11. What is wrong with threatening someone? What are some subtle or overt threats we might make?

12. What are a few examples of how you might persuade those under your charge to respond without threatening them?

13. Explain the phrase "knowing that both their Master and yours is in heaven." Who are the masters that Paul is referring to?

14. Identify two truths from these verses that can help you in your daily life. State what phrase or verse they originate from and what changes you need to make in your own life.

- 

-

# Advanced Study Questions for Ephesians 6:5-9

1. A slave's challenges differ from the average person today who is free. A slave cannot do what he or she wants. What advice does Paul give that helps clarify how both a slave and a master are to respond to their respective masters?

2. Should we apply these verses to our lives? (Most of us are not slaves.) If so, how?

3. In what ways are the masters of slaves similar to the slaves?

4. The scriptures tell us that He will reward those things rightly done "as to Christ." So what makes a term paper or washing a pile of dark clothes "as to Christ"? What attitude needs to be present? What if we are not aware of Jesus? Be specific as possible.

5. Obedience is very important. Through this arrangement the Lord will reward those who faithfully obey Him. Is there any area in which you are not obedient? Is what we gain in the short term by lazy attitudes or disobedience of more worth than what God would otherwise reward us for in eternity?

**BOOK OF EPHESIANS: BIBLE STUDIES**
*Living in the Heavenlies*

# Ephesians 6:10-13
## ENGAGED IN WAR

Saved? Yes. Loved? Yes. Protected? Yes. But still the apostle likens our life in this world to spiritual warfare.

➡ Do you think of your Christian life as a warfare? Explain why or why not.

## Basic Study Questions on Ephesians 6:10-13

> [10] Finally, be strong in the Lord, and in the strength of His might. [11] Put on the full armor of God, that you may be able to stand firm against the schemes of the devil. [12] For our struggle is not against flesh and blood, but against the rulers, against the powers, against the world forces of this darkness, against the spiritual forces of wickedness in the heavenly places. [13] Therefore, take up the full armor of God, that you may be able to resist in the evil day, and having done everything, to stand firm. (Eph 6:10-13)

1. The first word of Ephesians 6:10 is 'finally.' What has preceded this section for him to conclude in this way? Name at least eight topics that Paul has previously discussed in Ephesians.

2. What command is given in verse 10?

3. What do these phrases mean "strong in the Lord" and "strength of His might" (6:10)? Is there any difference between them? If so, what is it?

4. How does a person obey and "be strong in the Lord, and in the strength of His might" (6:10)?

5. What is the Ephesian church instructed to do in Ephesians 6:11?

6. What extra meaning might be added through the word "full" to armor (6:11)? What problem might Paul be addressing when he uses the term "full armor"?

7. Who provides us this armor (6:11)? Why is this important? How does this knowledge further help us?

8. For what purpose is the church instructed to put on the armor of God (6:11)?

9. What do we know about spiritual attacks from verse 11?

Ephesians 6:10-13 Engaged in War

10. In Ephesians 6:12, Paul first states that our struggle is not against flesh and blood. What does this mean?

11. From verse 12 list who our struggle is against? Do your best to identify what each might mean.

- _____
- _____
- _____
- _____

12. How does verse 12 help us better understand the difficulty we have in loving our neighbor?

13. Ephesians 6:13 is a powerful summary verse. If you had to separate this verse into parts, what would they be? (Four lines are available but they do not indicate the number of parts.)

- _____
- _____

- _____

- _____

14. What might the 'evil day' in verse 13 refer to?

15. By examining 6:13 do you think we can stand firm against the evil one?

16. What is one of your strong points and one of your weaknesses?

## Advanced Study Questions for Ephesians 6:10-13

1. Do you think these admonitions are applicable to today's church? If so, how?

2. Can you identify one or more schemes the evil one is using in today's world? Please explain.

3. Most people believe that it is the people around us that are the source of our problems (such as our spouse, roommate, neighbor, boss, etc.) rather than spiritual forces Paul discusses. What is really the case? How should we look at our circumstances in light of this?

# Ephesians 6:10-13 Engaged in War

4. What do you believe about spiritual forces? What difference does your belief make in the way you carry out your Christian life?

5. In what ways do you stand firm? When do you give in? What can you do about the latter?

## BOOK OF EPHESIANS: BIBLE STUDIES
Living in the Heavenlies

# Ephesians 6:14-17
## SPIRITUAL ARMOR

Most of us have probably heard about spiritual armor but are not quite sure how to fit such armor into our modern lives, much like young David trying to put King Saul's armor on and using it. Paul gives us much needed guidance about spiritual armor in this passage.

➡ What is one of your most vulnerable places? What makes it so?

## Basic Study Questions on Ephesians 6:14-17

> 14 Stand firm therefore, HAVING GIRDED YOUR LOINS WITH TRUTH, and HAVING PUT ON THE BREASTPLATE OF RIGHTEOUSNESS, 15 and having shod YOUR FEET WITH THE PREPARATION OF THE GOSPEL OF PEACE; 16 in addition to all, taking up the shield of faith with which you will be able to extinguish all the flaming missiles of the evil one. 17 And take THE HELMET OF SALVATION, and the sword of the Spirit, which is the word of God. (Eph 6:14-17)

1. What is the difference between "stand firm" and simply to stand (6:14)? Why is standing firm needed?

2. In verses 14-17 Paul lists numerous ways to help us stand firm and withstand the attack against us. Briefly state what they are.

3. What might be a more up-to-date way of stating, "girded your loins with truth" (6:14)? What is being conveyed? How does truth help us in our spiritual fight?

4. What was the breastplate used for in ancient fighting (6:14)? What is the modern name and use for this piece of equipment (perhaps think of how a policeman is outfitted)?

5. How does righteousness shield a person's faith (6:14)? How does unrighteousness make a person vulnerable? Do you think the enemy knows where the weaknesses are in your armor?

6. Good footwear in fighting is critical. How do good boots help one in fighting (6:15)? How would poor footwear hinder a person's chances of winning a fight?

7. How does the gospel of peace act as good footwear (6:15)?

8. How does the shield differ from the breastplate (6:16)? How does faith act as a shield?

Ephesians 6:14-17 Spiritual Armor

9. What is the shield of faith able to extinguish (6:16)? What difference does the word "all" make here? Explain and give at least two examples of how faith can help us in our daily lives.

10. From the way the enemy targets our weaknesses, what can we conclude about him, his power and his strategy from verse 16?

11. What are the last two ways Paul desires us to stand firm in verse 17? (Note: some would include prayer in verse 18, but we have included that in the next section focused on prayer.)

12. What part does the helmet play in a soldier's armor (6:17)? How does salvation/redemption serve as the helmet in our spiritual struggles?

13. What part does the sword play in the soldier's activity (6:17)? Do you agree that the sword is the only offensive part of his armor? What are the spiritual implications of this and how does the Word of God serve as a sword?

14. Look back at your Christian growth in the last six months. Would you say you are growing spiritually, staying the same or backsliding? Were you standing firm? In what area of your life do you suffer the most severe attack(s)? How can you regroup and stand firm?

15. Have you ever put each piece of spiritual armor on through prayer? Pray through the overall goal to stand firm and then seek the Lord to help you properly put on each piece of armor, paying special attention to particular insights the Spirit gives you while praying.

# Advanced Study Questions for Ephesians 6:14-17

1. Notice the capitalized words in this section of verses. Find where they are being quoted from in the Old Testament. Relate any new insights.

2. How do we further acquire truth to be all the more ready and mobilized to face the enemy (6:14)? Have you memorized scripture lately? Do you regularly meditate on God's Word? Start with these verses here.

3. Armor is only as good as its weakest point—does yours have gaps or holes? What area do you struggle with? Make an honest assessment and spend the next three months praying, studying and firming up your commitment to live a godly life.

4. Doubts allow enemy missiles to penetrate our hearts and minds. Seek the Lord in what areas doubts weaken you—concerning your assurance of salvation, ability to walk uprightly, holding back your temper, staying faithful to your wedding vows, your faith in the integrity of God's Word, etc. Remember God wants to build up your faith to withstand all those missiles. Seek Him for a plan to build up your faith and eliminate your doubts.

5. Study the relationship between the Spirit of God and the Word of God. Hint: Start with Eph 6:17 and continue with other NT verses: 1 Peter 1:22-25. John 3:5-6; 1 Cor 2:14-16. The Word of God only can be effectively applied to our lives through the Spirit of God.

**BOOK OF EPHESIANS: BIBLE STUDIES**
*Living in the Heavenlies*

# Ephesians 6:18-24
## POWER IN PRAYER

Although we may intellectually agree that prayer is important, our lack of prayer makes it quite evident that we do not believe in its effectualness or importance in our lives. What holds back God's people from serious and believing prayer? Learn about the power in prayer!

➡ What is one of the biggest problems you face in intercessory prayer? Why?

## Basic Study Questions On Ephesians 6:18-24

> [18] With all prayer and petition pray at all times in the Spirit, and with this in view, be on the alert with all perseverance and petition for all the saints, [19] and pray on my behalf, that utterance may be given to me in the opening of my mouth, to make known with boldness the mystery of the gospel, [20] for which I am an ambassador in chains; that in proclaiming it I may speak boldly, as I ought to speak. [21] But that you also may know about my circumstances, how I am doing, Tychicus, the beloved brother and faithful minister in the Lord, will make everything known to you. [22] And I have sent him to you for this very purpose, so that you may know about us, and that he may comfort your hearts. [23] Peace be to the

brethren, and love with faith, from God the Father and the Lord Jesus Christ. 24 Grace be with all those who love our Lord Jesus Christ with a love incorruptible. (Eph 6:18-24)

1. What is Paul speaking about in the passage before this one? (Look at 6:10-17.)

2. How is this passage connected to the former?

3. When does Ephesians 6:18 say we are to pray? What does this practically mean?

4. What two words describe how we are to pray (Eph 6:18)? What is the difference between them?

5. What does it mean to pray "in the Spirit" (Eph 6:18)? Is it "spirit" or "Spirit"? (Both are possible.)

6. What are we told to do at the end of Ephesians 6:18? What does this mean? Why is it important?

Ephesians 6:18-24 Power in Prayer    161

7. Is it wrong to pray for oneself? What does Paul ask us to do for him in Ephesians 6:19? How does this compare with how you pray for yourself?

8. Why did Paul want prayer (Eph 6:20)? How might this add special meaning to the former question of whether it is right to pray for oneself?

9. Who does the Apostle Paul mention in Ephesians 6:21-22? Why? What are two characteristics of this brother?

10. What are the two things Paul asks God for on behalf of the brethren in Ephesus (6:23)? What do these phrases mean? How would this help the church?

11. What does he ask for in Ephesians 6:24? What does this word mean? Be practical.

12. For whom does the apostle ask for these things (6:24)? Why?

13. What is the difference or similarity between a "love for God" and a "love incorruptible" (6:24)?

14. There are two applications for our lives in this section. Which is more difficult for you?

- Do you specifically pray for others? For whom? For what things do you intercede?

- Do you sense your need for prayer in such a way that it compels you to seek others to pray for you?

## Advanced Study Questions for Ephesians 6:18-24

1. Prayer is a crucial Christian discipline. There are set times of prayer and also 'an attitude of prayer' ("pray at all times in the Spirit"). What set times of personal prayer do you have? When do you pray with others through the week? Are there any improvements you need to make?

2. Regarding the phrase "pray at all times in the Spirit" (6:18), describe how one can pray through the day as one sees needs arise. Give some practical examples.

3. Prayer requests are special ways to fight the enemy. Can rumors masquerade as prayer requests? How should they be treated differently from a prayer request?

4. From the frequency with which you pray and the passion and kind of prayers that you bring before God, evaluate what you really believe about prayer. (For example, if I do not pray every day, I really believe

that prayer is not necessary for each day. If I really did believe it was crucial, then I would pray each day.)

# Appendix 1: Bible Study Chart[1]

| | Bible Passage | Study Title | Date |
|---|---|---|---|
| 1 | Ephesians 1:1-3 | Living as Saints | |
| 2 | Ephesians 1:4-6 | Chosen and Precious | |
| 3 | Ephesians 1:7-10 | A Grand World View | |
| 4 | Ephesians 1:11-14 | A Glorious Life | |
| 5 | Ephesians 1:15-17 | A Model of Prayer | |
| 6 | Ephesians 1:18-23 | Penetrating Prayers | |
| 7 | Ephesians 2:1-3 | The Need for Grace | |
| 8 | Ephesians 2:4-7 | God's Great Mercy | |
| 9 | Ephesians 2:8-10 | God's Awesome Plan for You | |
| 10 | Ephesians 2:11-18 | He Himself is Our Peace | |
| 11 | Ephesians 2:19-22 | No Longer Strangers | |
| 12 | Ephesians 3:1-10 | The Purpose of the Gospel | |
| 13 | Ephesians 3:11-19 | God's Greater Purposes | |
| 14 | Ephesians 3:20-21 | Extraordinary Glory | |
| 15 | Ephesians 4:1-3 | Preserving the Unity | |
| 16 | Ephesians 4:4-10 | Unity and Harmony | |
| 17 | Ephesians 4:11-16 | God's Goal for the Church | |
| 18 | Ephesians 4:17-24 | Life Transformation | |
| 19 | Ephesians 4:25 | Pure Living (Part 1) | |
| 20 | Ephesians 4:26-32 | Pure Living (Part 2) | |
| 21 | Ephesians 5:1-7 | Pure Living (Part 3) | |
| 22 | Ephesians 5:8-14 | Children of Light | |
| 23 | Ephesians 5:15-21 | Filled With the Spirit | |
| 24 | Ephesians 5:22-30 | Improving One's Marriage | |
| 25 | Ephesians 5:31-33 | The Picture of Marriage | |
| 26 | Ephesians 6:1-4 | Family Matters | |
| 27 | Ephesians 6:5-9 | Responsibilities and Opportunities | |
| 28 | Ephesians 6:10-13 | Engaged in War | |
| 29 | Ephesians 6:14-17 | Spiritual Armor | |
| 30 | Ephesians 6:18-24 | Power in Prayer | |

---

[1] Download chart at: www.foundationsforfreedom.net/dl/bibnt/NT_Pauline/Ephesians/ebs/Ephesians-Study-Chart.pdf

# Appendix 2: About the Author

Paul has worked as an overseas church planter during the 1980s and pastored in America during the 1990s. God called him to establish Biblical Foundations for Freedom in 2000 and since then he has been actively writing, holding international Christian leadership training seminars and serving in the local church.

Paul's wide range of books and media-rich training resources on Christian life, discipleship, godly living, leadership training, marriage, parenting, anxiety, Old and New Testament and other spiritual life topics provide special insights that are blended into his many books and media-rich training resources.

Paul has been married for more than thirty-five wonderful years. With eight children and three grandchildren, Paul and his wife Linda continually see God's blessings unfold in their lives.

For more on Paul and Linda and the BFF ministry, check online at : www.foundationsforfreedom.net

www.ingramcontent.com/pod-product-compliance
Lightning Source LLC
Chambersburg PA
CBHW071505040426
42444CB00008B/1497